THE

DOCTRINE OF BAPTISM,

AS TAUGHT IN THE

HOLY SCRIPTURES,

AND HELD BY

THE PROTESTANT EPISCOPAL CHURCH.

WRITTEN FOR THE PROTESTANT EPISCOPAL SOCIETY FOR THE PROMOTION OF EVANGELICAL KNOWLEDGE.

NEW-YORK:
PROTESTANT EPISCOPAL SOCIETY FOR THE PROMOTION OF EVANGELICAL KNOWLEDGE,
11 BIBLE HOUSE, ASTOR PLACE.

1854.

JOHN A. GRAY,
STEREOTYPER AND PRINTER,
95 & 97 Cliff street, N. Y.

THE

DOCTRINE OF BAPTISM.

THE MINISTRATION OF THE SPIRIT.

"GOD is a Spirit; and they that worship Him, must worship Him in spirit and in truth."*

SUCH was the teaching of Him who spake as never man spake. In the midst of a people, blinded by carnal prejudices, inflated by self-righteousness, confident in their descent from Abraham, proud of their divinely-given religion, superstitiously rigid in their adherence to its rites and ceremonies, but sadly ignorant of the nature of true holiness, the Lord Jesus Christ bore witness to the truth. He stood forth among His countrymen, not less as a reprover than a Messiah. He vindicated the spirituality of religion in an age of formalism, exposed the worthlessness and hollowness of mere external obedience, denounced the prevailing confidence in ritual observances as a refuge of lies, called men from the shell of religion to the substance, traced sin through all

* John 4: 24.

its disguises, unveiled the hidden corruption of the heart, and would tolerate no plausible substitute for the faith, repentance, and love of the soul itself. Such doctrine was new, surprising, offensive, intolerable to a people whose boast was, "The temple of the Lord, the temple of the Lord, the temple of the Lord are we;" and the malignant enmity and envy of Priests and Pharisees was insatiate until Jesus Christ was crucified.

In the study of the new religion which names him as its Author, and for a right appreciation of his teachings, it is most important to bear in mind this marked characteristic of his ministry. The Saviour was constantly opposing an excessive reliance upon the ritual of religion, to the neglect and oblivion of its spirit and reality. And while he disencumbered the ancient faith of the corruptions and traditions wherewith it had become encrusted and hidden, he revealed the new faith, related to the former as is the substance to the shadow. The new and better covenant, which he sealed with his own blood, presented heavenly truth, not under the cumbrous drapery of Levitical institutions, but in its native clearness, simplicity and beauty. The object of his mission from God was not merely to ordain new ceremonies, substitute sacraments for sacrifices, a symbolic church for a symbolic temple, a Gentile instead of an Aaronic priesthood. Christianity was not to be Judaism reproduced, with a ritual outwardly modified, but a character not essentially changed. It should be light contrasted with obscurity, liberty as opposed to bondage, simplicity instead of gorgeous and complicated ritualism, freedom of access to the Holiest instead of distance and barriers, a light yoke and easy burden in place of that system which, however indispensable as a preparation for the Gospel, proved to the Jews, St. Peter being witness, a yoke which neither they nor their fathers were able to bear. The Gospel, contrasted with the Law, is "the Ministration of the Spirit," and therefore preëminently "glorious."*

In place, therefore, of the multiplied, burdensome, and imposing ceremonies of the former dispensation, the Saviour instituted two simple and impressive rites, and enjoined them upon all his disciples. These were in some degree parallel to the two symbolic Jewish ordinances, Circumcision and the Passover. In the case of each, the acts prescribed, and invested with religious significance, were not previously unknown. Like the two previous ordinances, one was initiatory and single, applied to individuals, and not admitting repetition. The other was constant and social. Besides their other important uses, they visibly represented and exhibited two cardinal doctrines of the new faith: the cleansing of the soul from the pollution of sin by the Holy Ghost, and the taking away of guilt by the atoning sacrifice of the Lamb of God, offered once for all. Thus were held up before man the two great essentials to salvation, pardon and holiness. "This is He that came by water and blood."†

* 2 Cor. 3: 8. † 1 John 5: 6.

BAPTISM.

THE first of these ordinances, that which is parallel to Circumcision, the badge of discipleship, the initiation into the visible fold of Christ, is known as Baptism. It was practised during the Saviour's personal ministry, by his disciples acting under their Lord's direction,* and was by him enjoined, in his parting commission to his Apostles to evangelize the world, with the utmost solemnity.† From the occasional notices found in the Acts of the Apostles, and in the Epistles, we can not doubt that this command was invariably and scrupulously obeyed. From the Scriptures may be gathered the following particulars respecting this holy rite.

1. Its universal obligation upon all who would be Christians.

2. The requirement in the case of adults of spiritual qualifications, namely, repentance and faith, prior to the reception of the rite.‡

3. The unprofitableness thereof to such as received it without suitable dispositions.§

4. That Baptism was the outward visible sign of spiritual regeneration.‖

5. That Baptism is the seal of the forgiveness of sins to the penitent.¶ Not the actual channel of

* John 4 : 1, 2. † Matt. 28 : 19; Mark 16 : 16.

‡ Acts 2 : 38; 8 : 37; 10 : 47; 16 : 14, 15, 30–33.

§ Case of Simon, Acts 8 : 21.

‖ John 3 : 5; Rom. 6 : 3, 4; Col. 2 : 12.

¶ Acts 2 : 38; 22 : 16.

pardon, but the pledge of a pardon already granted to the believing.*

6. That the ordinance, and the grace which it exhibits and symbolizes, are not inseparable.†

7. That infants are proper subjects of baptism. "Suffer the little children to come unto me, and forbid them not; for of such is the kingdom of God."‡ We must understand "the kingdom of God" here, either of the Church of God on earth, or of the heavenly state. If the former be meant, the question is settled at once in favor of infant baptism. If the latter, is it credible that they, who are the proper heirs of heaven, were to be excluded from the Church below?—that they who are admissible into the inner sanctuary, can not be received into the vestibule and outer court of the temple? Congruous with this interpretation of our Saviour's words was the language of the Apostle Peter at Pentecost. "The promise is to you and to your children;"§ that of St. Paul, that when one parent is a Christian, the children are "holy;"‖ the record of the baptism of households in

* John 5 : 24; 5 : 40 compared with 6 : 35. Acts 11 : 15–17; 16 : 31; Rom. 4 : 1–12; 5.

† Simon received the ordinance, but not the grace. Cornelius and his friends were baptized with the Holy Ghost, before being baptized with water. 1 Cor. 10 : 1–5, compared with verse 11.

‡ Mark 10 : 14.

§ Acts 2 : 39.

‖ 1 Cor. 7 : 14. The word *holy* here is understood to mean not inherent but relative holiness, capable of dedication to God in his covenant.

three instances;* the usage in the Jewish Church, under the parallel rite of circumcision, and the practice of the Christian Church in the primitive ages.

REGENERATION.

To understand the true nature of Baptism, as it is presented in the Scriptures, and held by the Protestant Episcopal Church, it is indispensable to have clear, definite, and Scriptural views of Regeneration. Much confusion and contradiction, in relation to the sacrament, may be ascribed to unsettled or erroneous opinions on this point. "Except a man be born again," said our Lord Jesus Christ, "he can not see the kingdom of God." The absolute necessity of this new birth cannot therefore be questioned by one who credits the word of God. It is also evident from the Scriptures that to be blessed hereafter, men must be the subjects, in this life, of a thorough spiritual change, a transformation of character, a new creation in righteousness and true holiness. This necessity is also absolute, and arises from the innate sinfulness of men, the fault and corruption of our common nature. Man lost, at the Fall, the holy image of his Maker, the moral and spiritual likeness to God, and perfect conformity to the Divine will in which he was originally created. In the account of the birth of Seth, it is written, "Adam begat a son in his own likeness, *after his image.*" Adam was

* Acts 16 : 15, 33; 1 Cor. 1 : 16.

himself created in *the image of God.* But Seth was born in the image of his fallen parent. And this is true of every one born since into the world, except the holy child Jesus. But it is a truth as conformable to reason, as it is plainly taught in Scripture, that "without holiness no man shall see the Lord." For the enjoyment of His presence, and admission into his kingdom of glory, our unholy souls must be new created, and "as we have borne the image of the earthy," "the first Adam," we must "bear the image of the heavenly," "the second Adam, the Lord from heaven." To restore us to holiness and everlasting life was the object of our Saviour's mission into this sinful world. And by the moral transformation and sanctification of our souls, is his merciful design eventually accomplished. "He gave himself for us, that he might redeem us from all iniquity, and purify unto himself a peculiar people, zealous of good works."* The Agent through whom the Lord effects this change in the hearts of sinners is the Holy Spirit.

Upon these points there is no difference of opinion among members of the Protestant Episcopal Church. But when we come to the manner of this new creation, and the application of this grace to the soul, there is very material and important difference. The question whether the above moral and spiritual transformation takes place in the sacrament of baptism, is one that has for years greatly divided and

* Titus 2 : 14.

agitated the Church. It is felt, on the side of those who affirm, and of those who deny this proposition, to be of the very highest importance. The point in dispute is radical. There can be nothing gained by glossing it over with ambiguous phraseology. It must be met. It ought to be understood. Every intelligent Episcopalian should acquaint himself with this controversy, should form an opinion upon it, and should have fixed and well-defined views of the teaching of the Scriptures, and of the formularies of his own Church on this subject. The object of the present essay is to assist the inquirer in answering this exceedingly important question: Is it the doctrine of the Bible and of our own Church that the change of our sinful nature, without which we can not enter heaven, takes place invariably in Baptism? Or does it then take place invariably in the case of infants? For the more cautious advocates of this opinion seem now disposed to narrow the assertion to the case of baptized infants, admitting that in adults the blessing is contingent and conditional. Is then the moral transformation of the soul by the Holy Ghost inseparable from the baptism of infants?

Of this question the affirmative is taken by the Church of Rome, and by a portion of the Church of England, and of the Protestant Episcopal Church in the United States. Instances in proof of this assertion will be hereafter adduced.

An essential preliminary to the discussion of this question is to ascertain previously the meaning of the word, Regeneration. Is it that moral and spiritual change, of which we have already spoken? Is it the implanting of that new and holy nature without which we can not be saved? Is the new birth synonymous with "the death unto sin and the new life unto righteousness," with "the renewing of our minds," with "the new creation in Christ Jesus?"

"Except a man be born again, he can not see the kingdom of God." "Without holiness no man shall see the Lord."* Do these passages point the same way? And is regeneration the commencement of holiness in the soul? Or is regeneration something distinct from the spiritual renewal; an ecclesiastical, not a moral change? a transition from the world to the Church, accompanied with new privileges, helps and responsibilities, but not involving any change in the character of the soul? The latter was, a few years since, the meaning usually given to the word by those who called themselves High Churchmen, and upon this was based their explanation of the baptismal service of the Church. The assertion that they confounded the outward transition with the inward transformation, was often denied as a misconception of their system, and resented as a calumny. The spiritual change they called *Renovation*, distinguished it from the ecclesiastical change to which alone they would restrict the word *Regeneration*, and often insisted with much earnestness and faithfulness upon the necessity of spiritual renewal in case of the baptized. This explanation seemed to reduce the bap-

* Heb. 12 : 14.

tismal controversy to a question of words, and fostered the very common opinion that the difference, after all, was but nominal, the two parties being substantially agreed.* But the misapplication of

* Bishop Hobart's Sermons on Titus 3 : 5, Works, vol. 2. "The benefits of baptism and its final efficacy are suspended on conditions, which may be all summed up in the two of repentance and faith. All baptized persons, therefore, must exercise repentance and faith, or they forfeit the privileges of baptism. Now, the renunciation of sin, and this lively faith producing holy obedience, constitute that spiritual change which our Church enforces, particularly in the baptismal office, when she prays concerning those who are baptized, that 'the old Adam may be so buried that the new man may be raised up in them," etc. "It is worthy of remark how admirably, on this subject, the Church employs and amplifies the language of Scripture in which this spiritual change is denoted by 'being transformed by the renewing of the mind; by crucifying the flesh with the affections and lusts; by walking not after the flesh, but after the Spirit;' 'by putting off the old man with his deeds, and putting on the new man, which is renewed in knowledge after the image of him who created him.' This is the change of heart which is called, in Scripture, 'the renewing of the Holy Ghost,' becoming 'a new creature;' and in the correct language of systematic divinity, *renovation* or *sanctification*." pp. 469, 471.

To this most important change Bishop Hobart denies the just application of the word Regeneration. He censures Dr. Barrow and Tillotson for such use of the word. "From a want of precision, indeed, in the use of terms, these divines use the term regeneration as synonymous with sanctification and renovation; and thus afford an opportunity to the adversaries of baptismal regeneration of enlisting them in their cause, by quoting those passages in which the word is used in its popular but erroneous signification." p. 468.

"Regeneration is a change of our spiritual condition, a translation into a state in which our salvation is rendered possible. Renovation is that change of heart and life by which salvation is finally attained." p. 472.

scriptural language is not a harmless and indifferent things. Words are things. The selection of certain words by the Holy Spirit to express divine truths is not to be deemed immaterial, neither is inspired phraseology a matter of indifference. We are not safe in giving up the nomenclature of Scripture, under the impression that we retain the substance of its teaching. The history of the baptismal question may warn us, how much the cause of truth may be jeoparded and damaged by what were supposed to be mere verbal concessions. Of late, there has been a tendency to interpret the word, Regeneration in the broadest sense, as including both a change of state and a change of nature. Many probably who adopt the extreme view of this subject are not aware of the magnitude of this change.* Whether the advocates of baptismal regeneration were formerly always consistent with themselves, I do not now propose to inquire. My own impression is that they were by no means so. But the explanation above named greatly nullified or diminished objection to the doctrine. The present aspect of the case is, however, materially different. The conviction has been

* When Bishop Mant's Tract on this subject, propounding the dogma of inseparable baptismal regeneration, and stating that, "If the work of regeneration is not effected in baptism, it is almost impossible for any sober man to say when and by what means it is effected," was published by the "Society for Promoting Christian Knowledge," it was found necessary to change very materially the language of former publications of the same Society in order to avoid the manifest contradiction of their teaching.

growing that, both in the Scriptures and in the Prayer-Book, the meaning of the word can not be restricted to a mere ecclesiastical change. And the ground is now broadly taken, and advocated in books, catechisms, tracts, etc., prepared by societies calling themselves general societies of the Protestant Episcopal Church, that every baptized infant is in the highest sense spiritually regenerate, and that no such thing as regeneration is to be required or looked for after baptism. To question this dogma, it is alleged by some of its advocates, is a heresy. It is to discard the true interpretation of our baptismal service, and to deny an article of the Nicene creed.

The question is of the most important and practical character, mingling itself with pastoral instruction and parental duty. And if the view, which identifies the spiritual renewal with the baptismal washing be untrue and unscriptural, then we can easily perceive that it must be an error disastrous in its consequences. Multitudes must be thereby deceived, filled with false confidence, rendered secure of their future happiness while still dead in trespasses and sins, and live and die unconscious of that great change without which our Saviour declares that a man can not enter the kingdom of God.

We return to the question, What is Regeneration? Regeneration is, in its true Scriptural sense, *a spiritual change*, a new creation of the soul, a death unto sin, and a new birth unto righteousness, a radical heart-transformation, the introduction into the depraved soul of a new principle of holiness, a participation in the Divine nature.*

There can be, I conceive, no fairer and better mode of ascertaining what regeneration really implies, than by making St. John his own interpreter. In his Gospel is found the distinct and emphatic enunciation of this truth by the Saviour of the world. There the doctrine is propounded with clearness and authority, and all who listen to the teachings of Christ are assured that, "Except a man be born again, he can not see the kingdom of God." St. John, who, alone of the four Evangelists, has narrated this important and instructive conversation of our Lord with Nicodemus, must be supposed to have rightly understood his own language. Had he been an uninspired writer, this would be a reasonable inference. But as one who was guided and illuminated by the Spirit of Truth, it can not be gainsaid. It is not a little remarkable that the phrase which was introduced by our Lord in this conference with the Jewish Rabbi, is used by St. John, in his first epistle, with unusual frequency. The use of it is one of the marked features of that Epistle, and relied on by critics as one of the strong evidences that the Gospel and the Epistle are from the same author.† The expression is employed also in the Epistle in a very

* "Yet the infection of nature doth remain in them that are regenerated." Article 9. Hence the life-long conflict in the renewed heart, between the flesh and the Spirit; and sanctification progressive, and this side the grave imperfect.

† Horne's Introduction. i. 108.

particular, discriminating, and practical manner. Regeneration is presented in connection with certain dispositions and conduct; so presented that Christians may be enabled to apply to themselves the passages in which it occurs, in the duty of self-examination, and thus ascertain whether they are or are not regenerate. Now, if it be true that our Lord teaches that baptism implies and conveys regeneration, it would be enough for the Christian to know that he was baptized by one authorized to administer the sacrament. But the language of St. John in his Epistle is as different from any thing like this as possible. Among all the tests which he lays down of a regenerate state, there is *not a word* touching the sacrament of Baptism. Let us compare his teaching in the Epistle, with his record of the words of Christ in the Gospel:

"If ye know that he is righteous, ye know that every one that doeth righteousness is born of him." 1 John 2 : 29.

"Whosoever is born of God, doth not commit sin; for his seed remaineth in him; and he can not sin because he is born of God. In this the children of God are manifest, and the children of the devil." 3 : 9, 10.

"We know that we have passed from death unto life, because we love the brethren. He that loveth not his brother abideth in death." 3 : 14.

"Every one that loveth is born of God, and knoweth God." 4 : 7.

"Whosoever believeth that Jesus is the Christ, is born of God." 5 : 1.

"For whatsoever is born of God overcometh the world: and this is the victory that overcometh the world, even our faith." 5 : 4.

"We know that whosoever is born of God sinneth not; but he that is begotten of God keepeth himself, and that wicked one toucheth him not." 5 : 18.

From this Epistle, then, we learn these marked characteristics of the regenerate. They do not sin, (deliberately and habitually.) They are deterred from sin by the holy principle, the incorruptible seed received in their new birth. They are animated with fervent love towards the Saviour and his people. Their faith in the Saviour is genuine, living, and of power to overcome the temptations of an ensnaring, and the terrors of a persecuting world. They keep themselves, through Divine grace, against the wiles of the Wicked One.

Can we doubt, after such an exposition, the meaning of the word? Could more emphatic language be employed?

Compare St. John's description of Regeneration with the language of Bishop Hobart: "It is much to be lamented that many divines of the Church of England have fallen into the modern error, which originated in the Calvinistic school, of applying the word, *Regeneration*, to denote the work of grace on the heart, the operations of the Divine Spirit in forming holy affections in the soul, and in leading us to newness of life. This most important and essential change, which in Scriptural and primitive language is termed the renewing of the Holy Ghost—renovation—many excellent and orthodox divines of our own Church, following, unfortunately, the fashion of the times, style, "Regeneration."*

How came the Apostle John to fall into this modern error of the Calvinistic school?

The definers of regeneration, in the sense given in the above quotation, urge upon the baptismally regenerate the necessity of a subsequent conversion or renovation. "In order to this renovation, it is requisite that every baptized person should cherish a strong and lively sense of his need of this change of heart and life. A deficiency in this sensibility is a fundamental and most dangerous defect."†

But while Christians need daily repentance, daily forgiveness, and constant recoveries from lapses into sin, (for "in many things we offend all,") what need is there of a thorough change of heart and life to one who already truly believes in Christ, doth not yield himself as the servant of sin, resists the tempter, whose faith worketh by love, and overcometh the world, and who is already passed from death unto life?

At the risk of being classed with modern errorists of the Calvinistic school, we prefer to hold with St. John in his estimate of what Regeneration really signifies. We accept him as the best possible com-

* Hobart's Works, ii. 465.

† Vol 2. 498.

mentator on the words of his blessed Lord—words which St. John himself was selected to communicate to the Church. And, following his instruction, we are irresistibly drawn to the conclusion that Regeneration, or the New Birth, is precisely that great spiritual and moral change whereby alone the soul of fallen man can be fitted for the presence of God and the kingdom of glory. The new birth, and the renewal of the soul in righteousness, are equally indispensable, because they are one and the same thing. And the other signification of the word seems to have been accepted in order to harmonize the language of the Fathers upon the subject of baptism with truth and Scripture; and to obviate a supposed difficulty in the offices of our Church.

Other passages bearing upon this subject, which will be presently considered, will be found, on careful examination, to confirm this view. And if any other texts appear, at first glance, obscure, or even favorable to the other interpretation of the word, (as it is claimed by Bishop Hobart that Titus 3 : 5, is,) let it be borne in mind that the language of St. John's Epistle is positive and unambiguous. His words can not be tortured into a different sense. Text upon text, each alike clear and definite, exhibit his view of Regeneration. They are susceptible of no other natural and consistent interpretation. And since Scripture can not contradict itself, we are bound to interpret other texts, (like that in the Epistle to Titus,) so as not to conflict with the incontrovertible teaching of St. John.

The Tractarian advocate for baptismal regeneration, at the present day, does not usually deny that regeneration implies the moral and spiritual change, the new creation of the soul. But his position is, and it is the key-note of his whole system, that this change takes place invariably and exclusively in baptism. The more cautious maintainers of this system, however, finding it impossible to parry the thrusts of such writers as Mr. Faber, are now disposed to limit the assertion to the case of infant baptism. This limitation is, in fact, inconsistent with much of their reasoning. It compels them to adopt, in the construction of the office for baptism of adults, the very hypothetical explanation, to which they object, as dishonest and evasive, when applied to the office for infant baptism. But, in spite of this inconsistency, they now, in most cases, admit that the baptized adult is not invariably regenerate. They resort to the old subtlety of the schoolmen, that the adult may, by positive unbelief, place an *obex* or hindrance in the way of the efficacy of the ordinance.* Some there are, indeed, who do not scruple to assert that Simon Magus himself was spiritually regenerate in baptism. But the more moderate, and because more moderate the more plausible and dangerous theory, restricts the invariable regeneration to the case of infants. Adults can not become regenerate

* This *obex* does not appear, according to them, to be the absence of living faith, but a willful, determined rejection of the extended blessing, a positive turning away from Christ and his grace.

except in baptism. They may or may not be regenerated in baptism. Infants certainly are. Not being morally responsible, they can not interpose the *obex*, and therefore the rite is to them infallibly accompanied with the new-creating energy of the Holy Spirit.

So much importance is attached to this view of Baptism by its maintainers, that the denial of it is considered by the present Bishop of Exeter, Dr. Philpotts, a sufficient reason for not consenting to the induction of a clergyman into a cure in his Diocese. And although his decision has been overruled by the highest judicial tribunal known to the Church of England, yet is it still, by himself, and by a large party who sympathize with him, adhered to with undiminished tenacity. The present Bishop of Ripon, Dr. Longley, has, it would seem, made assent to the same dogma a test of fitness for ordination.*

* Questions proposed to the Rev. Mr. Heyward by the examining chaplain of the Bishop of Ripon.

"Are you prepared to teach as the doctrine of the Church,

"1. That regeneration is the grace specially conferred in and by baptism, and that the term is not applicable to any grace bestowed before or after baptism?

"2. That regeneration is in such a manner attached to baptism, that it is withheld from no person baptized according to the due order of the Church, unless in case of willful impenitence and unbelief?

"3. That infants being incapable of willful impenitence and unbelief, ... every infant baptized is in and by baptism regenerated?"

Mr. Heyward was refused orders because not ready to answer these questions affirmatively.

"The very thing a Heathen moralist would most desire, such as the mortification of the flesh, the death unto sin, the creation of a new

The doctrine, therefore, is not only strongly maintained, but enforced, when its holders have the power, with the utmost intolerance. Had men like

spirit within us, the enlightenment of the mind, the admission into a noble spiritual polity, the cleansing of the conscience, the forgiveness of sins and restoration to the favor of God, or union with his nature, —all these are described in the Bible as effected by baptism already. It is something past and done, and the subsequent struggle, for struggle there must be, is to defend what we have received, to recover ourselves from falling from the high estate in which we have been placed."—*Sewell's Christian Morals*, p. 211.

The sermon of Bishop McCoskry, on the celebration of the Jubilee of "the Society for the Propagation of the Gospel in Foreign Parts," derives additional importance from the occasion of its delivery. It contains a very unequivocal and thorough-going enunciation of the extreme theory of Baptismal Regeneration. God "has given his own Son to be the head of a new family on the earth, the descendants of which are bound together by stronger ties than blood. They are, in the higher sense, brethren. They are connected through the Son of God. It becomes an important matter to inquire, in what manner are we admitted into this family, and thus made brethren? It is by baptism. This is the initiatory rite. No amount of personal holiness, (if it can be ever acquired out of this family,) or inward experiences, or raptures, can make us members of the Church of Christ. We must enter through the door which its Divine Head has opened, and we must enter by receiving, from those whom he has constituted, as his earthly representatives, the right to enter, and this right, we have observed, is baptism. In this ordinance every child is made a new creature in Christ Jesus. They are born again, both of water and of the Spirit. For this great, this mighty, this heavenly work, there are no qualifications required; and to guard against failures, the Spirit of God is given to every child in baptism, without any exception, not only to begin, but to carry on and complete the great work of their salvation. The relationship thus created will remain. It never can be shaken off in this world; however unworthy the members of this family may become, they will still remain the children of God.

"In adults, the terms are different. There is actual sin in connection the Bishops of Exeter and Ripon the control of the Church, hard indeed would be the condition of those who can not, with a good conscience, assent to this extravagant assumption. A large portion of the Church of England, and of the Protestant Episcopal Church in the United States, feel bound to deny its truth, and to protest against it as false, unproved by Scripture, and eminently dangerous.

The object of the present Tract is to examine this tenet; and to subject it to the test:

I. *Of the Word of God;*

II. *Of observation and experience;*

III. *Of the Articles, Homilies, and Offices of the Protestant Episcopal Church.*

with the sad inheritance of a fallen nature. Hence, there must be previous qualifications, and these are repentance, faith, and obedience, or, in other words, conversion. But this is not regeneration, or the new birth." See Sermon by Bishop McCoskry, and Appendix, C., p. 39, of Bishop De Lancey's Report of the Mission to the Jubilee.

"One may then define regeneration to be that act whereby God takes us out of our relation to Adam, and makes us actual members of his Son, and so his sons, as being members of his ever-blessed Son, and if sons, then heirs of God through Christ. This is our new birth, an actual birth of God, of water and the Spirit, as we were actually born of our natural parents; herein then also are we justified, or both accounted and made righteous, since we are made members of Him who is alone righteous; freed from past sin, whether original or actual; having a new principle of life imparted to us, since having been made members of Christ we have a portion of his life, or of him who is our life. . . . The view then here held of Baptism, following the ancient Church and our own, is that we be engrafted into Christ, and thereby receive a principle of life, afterwards to be developed and enlarged by the fuller influxes of his grace."—*Dr. Pusey, Tracts for the Times*, vol. 2, p. 24.

I. THE TRACTARIAN DOCTRINE OF BAPTISMAL REGENERATION TESTED BY THE WORD OF GOD.

The texts most relied on by its advocates are John 3 : 5, 6, and Titus 3 : 5. The former first claims our attention. "Except a man be born of water and of the Spirit, he can not enter into the kingdom of God." "That which is born of the flesh is flesh, and that which is born of the Spirit is spirit." To be born of water is assumed at once to mean Baptism. It is then argued that our Saviour speaks of but one new birth, and hence that whosoever is baptized is born both of water and of the Spirit, and that when born of water in the sacrament, he is also, *ex necessitate*, born of the Holy Ghost, and made a new creature in Christ Jesus.

Granting that being born of water is to be literally understood, and denotes the sacrament of baptism,* it is a most unwarrantable assumption to deduce therefrom the certainty that every baptized person is born again of the Spirit. If our Lord introduces here an allusion to baptism, he refers to it as an emblem of the spiritual new birth, an outward visible exhibition of that which must take place in the souls of his people. But what is the point, the object of

* This interpretation has the sanction of antiquity, and appears to be favored by our Church in the baptismal office. A passage remarkably parallel, however, Matt. 3 : 11, "He shall baptize you with the Holy Ghost and with fire," would seem to favor the figurative interpretation of the word *water*, as indicative of the cleansing and purifying influence of the Spirit upon the heart. Compare also Ezekiel 36 : 25–27.

this conversation? Is it to impress upon the mind of a Jewish Rabbi the indispensable necessity of an outward rite, or of inward holiness? Let us take into consideration the usual character of these men. How prone were they to exaggerate external observances! How greatly, in thein overweening estimate of the ceremonial and ritual, had they lost sight of what was spiritual and holy! Such an one, coming to Christ for instruction in the great things of his kingdom, is emphatically assured that to see, to enjoy, or to enter that kingdom, "a man must be born again." There would be a marvellous descent from the beginning to the close of our Lord's address, one wholly opposed to his usual style, if all that our Lord meant was, that to enter his visible Church, a man must be baptized. (Hobart's Works, Vol. II. p. 456.) Or if we understood him with the Tractarian as testifying, "In order to be true subjects of my kingdom and enjoy its eternal blessings, you must receive the sacrament of baptism, in which, of course, your soul will be new-created by the Holy Spirit, your unholiness purged, and your sins forgiven."

Surely, here is presented to the inquiring Jew a degree of virtue and efficacy in an outward rite, which Scribes and Pharisees never surpassed in their exaggeration of the Mosaic ceremonies. If this be our Lord's meaning, why is Nicodemus reproved for his want of acquaintance with the nature and blessings of this new ordinance? What opportunity had he enjoyed, as "a master of Israel," of knowing the importance and efficacy of Christian baptism? This, we may reasonably suppose, was the first time the Gospel had been unfolded to him. If our Saviour meant to convey the idea that his kingdom must be entered by a new rite, the application of water, with a certain form of words, and that the reception of this rite was to be of course accompanied with such a spiritual blessing that the recipient became a child of God and an heir of his kingdom, this need not so much surprise and startle him, for it was very much what the Scribes taught concerning circumcision. The difference between them and Jesus would then consist in little else than the substitution of baptism for circumcision. If, as some learned men tell us, the Jews at that period admitted proselytes from among the Gentiles by a water baptism, and called such proselytes *new born*, this custom must have been familiar to the Rabbi, and what was there then in Christ's address to occasion his evident astonishment and perplexity? The expressions of Nicodemus indicate a mind startled by some new and amazing proposition. Yet the truth which had thus affected and surprised him was one, our Saviour assures him, which ought to have been familiar to his mind, as a master of Israel. Would our Saviour speak thus of any truth which was not plainly taught in the Old-Testament Scriptures? Would he, who was so constantly and severely reproving the Jews of his day for neglecting and forsaking the word of God, and rendering it of none effect by their traditions, would he have drawn his language and illustrations from modern Rabbinic usage, and rebuked Nicodemus for his ignorance thereof? Either of these interpretations is plainly derogatory to our Saviour's character, and contradictory to the whole tenor of his teaching. But the doctrine of the necessity of a moral and spiritual change to fit sinful man for the favor, presence, and enjoyment of God, was one, however, overlooked by the Jews at that time, which was plainly taught in their own Scriptures. This change from sin to holiness was represented in the Old Testament as something not necessarily included in their outward rites, but as being the substance which they shadowed out. (Deut. 30 : 6; Ps. 51; Isa. 1 : 11–18; Jer. 31 : 33; Ezek. 11 : 19; 18 : 31; 36 : 25–27.) The devout student of the Psalms and Prophets could not fail to find it there. And the universal corruption of the nation was imputable to the ignorance of their professed guides and teachers of this and similar great verities.

The main thing, therefore, which our Saviour proposed to the inquiring Rabbi, was the indispensableness, to the enjoyment of his spiritual and eternal kingdom, of a new creation of the depraved and sin-loving soul. Upon this necessity he insisted as of universal application, and his whole demeanor and language are perfectly consistent with the magnitude and importance of his theme. If in his mention of water in connection with this new birth, he refers to the sacrament of baptism, he does so incidentally, inasmuch as the rite, which he had adopted for entrance into his visible Church, was designedly emblematic of the inward cleansing of the soul. In this view, the allusion is obviously appropriate. "Just as the proselyte to my religion is to be admitted into the company of my disciples by a sacramental ablution, so must every one, who shall here enjoy the first fruits, and hereafter fully inherit my salvation, be inwardly cleansed and purified by the Holy Ghost, and receive through its transforming energy a new nature." Our Saviour accordingly goes on to contrast the carnal nature and disposition of the unregenerate, with the spiritual capacities and character of those who have experienced this new birth. "That which is born of the flesh is flesh"; the natural man is unholy, sinful, and sensual. "That which is born of the Spirit is spirit." The new man is spiritually minded, and partakes of the holy tendencies of the Divine Regenerator. This doctrine ought not, continues our Lord, to excite your astonishment and surprise, for the presence of a Holy God, and the enjoyment of a holy kingdom, require a holy nature on the part of man. The new birth is to you in many respects inscrutable, for the Spirit, like the wind, "bloweth where it listeth." Its secret operation is beyond your control, or observation, or cognizance, while yet the effects are perceptible and observable. "You hear the sound thereof, but can not tell whence it cometh, nor whither it goeth." But if the new-creating Spirit accompany, as a matter of course, every ministration of the baptismal rite, then, so far from resembling the wind, which bloweth where it listeth, the Spirit is brought within the control, direction, and disposal of man. For man has it in his power to give or to withhold the baptismal rite. The reception of it in the case of infants depends upon the will of parents and sponsors, and of the officiating minister. And in this connection we can not but refer to John 1 : 12, 13, "The sons of God" are "born again, not of the will of the flesh, nor of the will of man, but of God." But if all the baptized are *ipso facto* born again, and made the sons of God, are they not born of the will of man? Their new birth depended, in the case of adults, on their own will, and in both adults and infants on the will of the dispenser of the ordinance.* Thus in direct contradiction to these emphatic assertions of Scripture, the dogma of the inseparable connection of spiritual regeneration with baptism makes man the dispenser of the Holy Ghost, and renders the new birth of the sons of God dependent on the will or caprice of a fellow-sinner. On the theory of inseparable baptismal regeneration, the blessed Trinity have so fettered and bound themselves, that they can not renew a soul in holiness until the priest ministers the baptismal ablution. Surely a consequence so replete with irreverence and blasphemy,

* Suppose, as in the case on Pitcairn's Island, in the midst of the Pacific Ocean, but a single ordained minister accessible to a community. On this interpretation of John 3, connected with the usually concomitant theory of the sole validity of sacerdotal baptism, the priest has under his control the salvation of the whole people. They can only be born again *of his will.*

ought to make men cautious in embracing a theological system which inevitably issues in it.*

Our Saviour pursues farther the discourse with Nicodemus, but not one syllable more do we hear on the subject of baptism. But, let it be noted, we do hear very much of *salvation by faith* in him. "As Moses lifted up the serpent in the wilderness, even so must the Son of Man be lifted up; that whosoever believeth in him should not perish, but have eternal life." Are we not at liberty, are we not bound by fair interpretation, to consider our Lord's subsequent language as connected with, and illustrative of, his previous affirmation? His subsequent words contain no allusion whatever to water or baptism, and in no way harmonize with the interpretation which makes baptismal regeneration the key-note of his discourse. But they do most perfectly harmonize with the opposite view, which makes the moral

* In perfect consistency with this arrogation to man of the power of dispensing the Divine Spirit, we find the following very exceptionable language occurring in a Tract which advocates this theory of Baptismal Regeneration. "As finally, we believe that from their first birth, they belong to human-kind, contain in themselves the germs of its distinctive character, and share mysteriously in its sin and woe, so we believe that, even at that unconscious age, WE CAN MAKE THEM CHRISTIANS BY A SECOND BIRTH, can impart to them in germ that sacred gift, which, duly tended and fostered, will counteract the poison of their nature, and transform them into the image of God. It is OUR PRIVILEGE, through the benefit of their second, to anticipate the growing evils that result from their first birth, and overcome them with good."—*Tract No.* 171.—Protestant Episcopal Tract Society, New-York.

and spiritual change, irrespective of outward rites, his great topic.

In verses 3–8 he testifies the necessity to salvation of a new birth by the Spirit. In verses 14–18, he declares that the manner of salvation is, through faith, directed towards himself, faith which might be compared to the gaze of the dying Israelite upon the serpent of brass. He affirms, most explicitly, the salvation of every sincere believer, and the condemnation of every unbeliever, and this without any reference whatever to any outward ordinance or observance. And the tenor of this discourse is also in perfect harmony with the passage just cited, John 1 : 12, 13, where, while the privilege of being sons of God by a new birth is declared to be the free gift of God, not dependent on the will of man, yet is it also assured to *all that believe on the name of Christ.* The two passages taken together present this new birth in inseparable union with faith. We can not but gather from them that *the believer is regenerate;* that *the unbeliever is unregenerate;* for as the new birth is indispensable to entrance into God's kingdom, so is faith in Jesus indispensable to salvation. And inasmuch as St. John testifies that the Saviour gave to such as believed on his name power to become the sons of God, he virtually denies this privilege to all others.

Compare also John 5 : 24 ; 1 John 5 : 1.

Aside, then, from the general testimony of Scripture, the fair interpretation of the first and third chapters of St. John's gospel is not consistent with the dogma that is attempted to be extorted from the single expression, "Except a man be born of water." And if our Saviour here introduces the necessity of an outward profession of his religion, in connection with an experience of its transforming power, as in Mark 16 : 16, "He that believeth and is baptized shall be saved," it would no more follow that regeneration is inseparable from baptism in the one case, than that faith is inseparable therefrom in the other. The utmost that can be justly inferred is, that God requires both. That the requirement in the one case is absolute, but not in the other, is further evident from the concluding words, "He that believeth not shall be damned." But no such awful penalty is annexed to the absence of baptism.

There is not the least difficulty in harmonizing with the above interpretation, Titus 3 : 5, "He saved us by the washing of regeneration, and the renewing of the Holy Ghost." Many commentators of note refer the former clause to baptism, and some prefer to render it "the laver of regeneration." Admitting this sense, the sacramental emblem is presented in connection with the spiritual change. But how is it that it saves us? Let St. Peter answer: "The like figure whereunto, even baptism, doth also now save us, (*not the putting away of the filth of the flesh*, but the answer of a good conscience towards God,) by the resurrection of Jesus Christ." 1 Pet. 3 : 21.*

* Note, moreover, that the Apostle denies salvation to "*works of righteousness* which we have done," and attributes it, in contrast with such works, to *the mercy of God*, extended through the washing of

But while the passage presents no difficulty, if we understand λουτρον to signify the baptismal washing or laver, another interpretation suits better the parallelism between the two clauses of the sentence, so marked a feature of Scripture style. "The washing of regeneration, and the renewing of the Holy Ghost." In the latter clause, *the Holy Ghost* is the efficient cause, *the renewing* the effect. The usage of parallelism would require us to regard *the regeneration* as the cause *the washing* as the effect, in the corresponding clause. Then the phrase here must be understood, not of the sacrament, but of spiritual regeneration, washing, and cleansing the soul. Another washing than that of water would then be meant.

EPH. 5:25–27.

In this passage is evidently contemplated the complete sanctification and glorious presentation of the

regeneration, etc. Are not sacramental observances to be reckoned among the works of righteousness, or good actions of the Christian? For his own baptism by John, the Saviour gave as the reason, "Thus it becomes us to fulfill all righteousness." No actions connected with religion can be indifferent. Performed as God requires, they are works of righteousness. If not so performed, they are sins. The Apostle has evidently in his mind the highest attainments of Christian holiness, for this gives force and emphasis to his denial. Either, then, the baptism of a sincere penitent is not a work of righteousness, an acceptable and holy act on his part, or the washing of regeneration here does not intend baptism. For what is just before denied to the works of righteousness, is affirmed of the washing of regeneration. Of course, the best actions of the Christian are devoid of merit, and are only acceptable through the mediation of Christ.

Bride of Christ to her Divine Spouse. The Church here spoken of is "the mystical body" of Christ, "the blessed company of all faithful people,"* "the general assembly and Church of the first born, whose names are written in heaven." The cleansing of this sanctified body is an ablution of which *the Word*, not the sacrament of baptism is the instrument. As this washing is effectual, not only to the cleansing of the Bride of Christ, but to present her a glorious and immaculate Church to her Lord, which will be accomplished at the marriage supper of the Lamb, we must admit the final salvation of all to whom it is applied. The strenuous advocates for baptismal regeneration are hardly prepared yet to maintain the universal salvation of the baptized, however their doctrine may gravitate in that direction.

Acts 22:16.

"And now, why tarriest thou? Arise, and be baptized, and wash away thy sins, calling on the name of the Lord."

We have already remarked, among the inferences from Scripture, that baptism was the appointed public pledge and seal of forgiveness to the penitent believer. Thus is he "baptized for the remission of sins," professing his penitence and renunciation of sin, and his faith in the pardoning mercy of God

* Collect for All-Saints' Day, and prayer in Post-Communion service.

through Christ. Thus before men and angels, the baptized person, giving "the answer of a good conscience," may be said to wash away his sins. But shall we gather from the text that St. Paul's sins were not forgiven by God until the moment of his baptism? If so, he expresses himself very strangely in the Epistle to the Romans, ch. 4. If he knew himself to be justified in and by baptism, it is inconceivable that he should be so solicitous to prove that all Christians are justified by faith alone, and especially that he should write as he did concerning the parallel ordinance of circumcision, and take such pains to prove that "Abraham's faith was reckoned unto him for righteousness, not in circumcision, but in uncircumcision," and that "he received the sign of circumcision, a seal of the righteousness of the faith which he had yet, being uncircumcised: That he might be the father of all them that believe, though they be not circumcised, that righteousness might be imputed unto them also." Circumcision was, as well as baptism, the sign of spiritual regeneration, and the seal of the righteousness of faith. Yet the Apostle considers it very important to his exhibition of the grace of the Gospel, to impress upon his readers that the thing signified in the case of Abraham preceded the sign. He had the grace before the ordinance. His faith was counted for righteousness, that is, he was justified before God, previously to his circumcision. And in this he was the father, the example, the pattern of future believers, Gentiles as well as Jews. Now, if the Apostle's reasoning did not apply under the new dispensation, as well as the old, to baptism as well as circumcision, it would be wholly irrelevant. He is certainly speaking of the justification of Christians, and in so doing, he argues that justification by faith, instead of being a new doctrine, was from the beginning. Is it possible that St. Paul, while insisting so strongly upon this great truth, and proving that Abraham was justified not in, or by virtue of, or at the time of his circumcision, but previously thereto, even as soon as he exercised genuine faith, knew all the while that he himself was not justified until the very moment of his baptism; that God's pardoning mercy was suspended in his own case until the sacramental washing; that he continued in his sins up to the instant of his baptismal regeneration? Such a fact, if fact it was, nullifies the whole of his reasoning from the example of Abraham, and renders that example altogether inapplicable to his Christian readers. The mention of it in this connection could only mislead and deceive them. What modern advocate of Baptismal Justification, reasoning thereupon, would take pains to show that the father of the faithful was as truly and fully justified before his circumcision, as he was after? Aside, therefore, from other obvious objections to the meaning which is attempted to be put upon Acts 22 : 16, the Apostle's own statements and reasonings in Romans 4, decisively refute it. Unless he knew himself justified before his baptism—and justification includes forgiveness—he could not, with a good conscience, have penned his exposition of that great doctrine of justification by faith in the Epistle to the Romans. When Ananias invited him to baptism, Paul was already blessed with the pardon, which was to be thus publicly and solemnly signed and sealed; and Ananias accordingly addresses him before his baptism as a brother.

Nothing is more common and natural, in addressing a body of men, than to take them to be what they profess to be, and to appeal to them by motives drawn from this profession. Such motives they can not gainsay or evade, but by discrediting their own solemn act. The Apostles, in addressing Christian churches, act upon this reasonable and prevalent principle. The converts to whom their epistles were written, had made a profession of their sincere repentance and faith in Jesus Christ, and this at a time when such an act exposed them to injury, contempt, and persecution. This profession was made in their baptism. We might expect to find the Apostles frequently reminding them of this solemn transaction, urging them with its whole weight of meaning, and appealing to them as really possessed of the spiritual qualifications demanded for that rite, and the spiritual blessings promised. Such is the easy, obvious import of such passages as Romans 6: 3, 4; Gal. 3: 27,* and Col. 2: 12, wherein Baptism is introduced

* In Gal. 3: 26–29, the Apostle is showing the equality of all that are in Christ, and denying any superiority to the Jew over the Gentile. "Ye are *all* the children of God, by faith in Christ Jesus."

in connection with the privileges, hopes, and duties of Christians. As the faith which united the soul to Christ, and made it partaker of his grace, was avowed in this ordinance, the Apostles very naturally address their baptized converts as sincere believers, in a state of grace and acceptance, and urge upon them the Christian obligations which they had publicly and voluntarily assumed. But, in so doing, they frequently interpose cautions against putting undue confidence in their outward privileges, and call them to faithful scrutiny of the heart and conduct.

But while all the texts on which the advocate for the inseparable connection of spiritual regeneration with baptism relies for scripture proof, are susceptible of a very natural and unconstrained explanation upon the evangelical view, that baptism is the sacramental sign and seal of regeneration, there are many passages that can not be harmonized, upon any fair principles of interpretation, with the former opinion, and which teach a doctrine plainly contrary thereto. To John 1 : 12, 13, and John 3, I have already adverted. All the spiritual blessings attributed to baptism are in other places clearly ascribed to faith, to prayer, and to the word of God as the instrument.

The maintainers of the dogma against which we protest assert that spiritual life is only communicated in baptism.

"For *as many of you* as have been baptized into Christ have put on Christ."

"There is neither Jew nor Greek," etc.

Saith our Lord Jesus Christ, "Verily, verily, I say unto you, He that heareth my word, and believeth on him that sent me, hath everlasting life, and shall not come into condemnation; but is passed from death unto life."* And St. John, "But these are written, that ye might believe that Jesus is the Christ, the Son of God: and that believing ye might have life through his name."† "To whom coming," saith St. Peter, "as unto a living stone, disallowed indeed of men, but chosen of God and precious, ye also, as lively stones, are built up a spiritual house, a holy priesthood," etc. 1 Peter 2 : 5, 6. The component parts, therefore, of this spiritual house are quickened, made living stones by coming to the chosen corner-stone—coming, that is, in faith.

They affirm that the Holy Ghost is *ex opere operato*, given in baptism.

Saith our Lord, "If any man thirst, let him come unto me and drink. He that believeth on me, as the scripture hath said, out of his belly shall flow rivers of living water. But this spake he of the Spirit, which they that believe on him should receive, for the Holy Ghost was not yet given, because that Jesus was not yet glorified."‡ "If ye, then, being evil, know how to give good gifts unto your children, how much more shall your Heavenly Father give the Holy Spirit to them that ask him?"§

It was announced as the peculiar prerogative of our Saviour that he should "baptize with the Holy

* John 5 : 24.
† John 20 : 31.
‡ John 7 : 37–39.
§ Luke 11 : 13.

Ghost." Has he made over this right to any mortal plenipotentiary? If so, when and in what terms? Until we have plain warrant for the stupendous grant, we must believe that the Lord retains, as head over all things to his Church, this divine prerogative.

St. Paul asks, "This only would I learn of you, Received ye the Spirit by the works of the law, or *by the hearing of faith?*" "That the blessing of Abraham might come on the Gentiles through Jesus Christ; that we might receive the promise of the Spirit through faith."*

The purifying of the heart they attribute to baptism. Saith St. Peter, "God bare them witness, giving them the Holy Ghost, even as he did unto us: and put no difference between us and them, purifying their hearts by faith."†

They say that baptism washes away sins. The forgiveness of sins is part of our justification. It would be superfluous to cite the numerous texts which establish the doctrine of justification by faith alone. Neither is it in the mouth of a member of the Protestant Episcopal Church to deny it, without the grossest inconsistency with his own standards. But if justified by faith alone, then are our sins forgiven when we turn to God through Christ in faith, *and not before.*

If it be urged that St. Peter exhorted the converts at Pentecost to be "baptized for the remission of sins,"‡

* Gal. 3: 2, 14. † Acts 15 : 8, 9.

‡ Collect for All-Saints' Day, and prayer in Post Communion Service.

so was the baptism of John for the remission of sins.* Were all baptized by John spiritually regenerated? If so, why were his disciples rebaptized?†

It is not baptismal water, but the blood of Christ, which washes away our sins,‡ and the application of that blood to our souls is by faith.

Baptism, it is said, makes us children of God. This is granted in one sense, inasmuch as it brings us into covenant with our Father in Heaven. So Israel, as a people, was God's son. But in the truest sense, we are made the children of God by faith in Jesus Christ. "But as many as received him, to them gave he power to become the sons of God, even to them that believe on his name: which were born not of blood, nor of the will of the flesh, nor of the will of man, but of God."§ "For he is not a Jew which is one outwardly; neither is that circumcision, which is outward in the flesh: but he is a Jew which is one inwardly; and circumcision is that of the heart, in the spirit, and not in the letter; whose praise is not of men, but of God."‖

The proof of sonship is the spirit of adoption in the heart, and a walk after the Spirit. "For as many as are led by the spirit of God, they are the sons of God."¶

Again, baptism is represented as the exclusive means of our union with Christ.

Such is not the teaching of the Saviour himself: "Behold, I stand at the door and knock; if any man

* Mark 1:4. † Acts 19:5. ‡ 1 John 1:7.
§ John 1:12, 13. ‖ Rom. 2:28, 29. ¶ Rom. 8:14, 15.

hear my voice and open the door, I will come in to him, and will sup with him and he with me."* Nor of St. Paul; "That He would grant you, according to the riches of his glory, to be strengthened with might by his Spirit in the inner man; that Christ may dwell in your hearts by faith."† Nor of St. John: "And he that keepeth his commandments dwelleth in him, and he in him. And hereby we know that he abideth in us, by the spirit which he hath given us."‡

Our Saviour's words in John 6:56, "He that eateth my flesh, and drinketh my blood, dwelleth in me, and I in him," are applied by the Church of Rome to the Eucharist; by Protestants almost universally to faith. In arguing with Protestants we may reasonably rely on this text to prove that union with Christ is the result not of baptism, but of faith.

Baptism is sometimes represented as the instrument or title of our resurrection to eternal life. "Jesus said unto her, I am the resurrection and the life: he that believeth in me, though he were dead, yet shall he live: and whosoever liveth, and believeth in me, shall never die."§

Without undertaking to limit the sovereign grace of God, or denying that he may new create the soul of an infant at the very moment of baptism, from Scripture testimony it is plain that the ordinary instrument of regeneration is *not the sacrament, but the word.*

* Rev. 3:20.
† Eph. 3:16, 17.
‡ 1 John 3:24.
§ John 11:25, 26.

The following are decisive texts.

John 17 : 17. "Sanctify them through thy truth; thy word is truth."

2 Peter 1 : 4. "Whereby are given unto us exceeding great and precious promises, that by these ye might be partakers of the divine nature, having escaped the corruption that is in the world through lust."

Participation in the divine nature is certainly regeneration. This is effected through the great and precious promises of the Gospel. How are promises to produce this effect in us but by being believed; that is, we become partakers of the Divine nature through faith in the promises; and so the Apostle continues—"Add to *your faith*, virtue."

James 1 : 18. "Of his own will begat he us with the word of truth."

1 Peter 1 : 22, 23. "Seeing ye have purified your souls in obeying the truth through the Spirit, unto unfeigned love of the brethren, see that ye love one another with a pure heart, fervently: being born again, not of corruptible seed, but of incorruptible, by the word of God which liveth and abideth for ever."

1 Cor. 4 : 15. St. Paul tells the Corinthians, "Though ye have ten thousand instructors in Christ, yet have ye not many Fathers; for in Christ Jesus I have begotten you through the Gospel."

If the Corinthians were born again in baptism, we should gather, of course, from these words, that the Apostle meant to say that he had administered to them this sacrament. But in chapter 1 : 14, 17, he tells them, "I thank God that I baptized none of you but Crispus and Gaius; lest any should say that I had baptized in mine own name." "For Christ sent me not to baptize, but to preach the Gospel."

Could St. Paul have thus expressed himself if he considered the spiritual new birth inseparable from baptism? His words can only be explained by the supposition that the Corinthians were regenerated *through his preaching unto them Christ crucified.* And from this passage we may gather also St. Paul's estimate of the comparative importance of the word and the sacraments in the economy of the Gospel. If spiritual life is only or chiefly communicated and sustained through the sacraments, then the sacramental functions of the Ministry are immeasurably the most important; and the proclamation of divine truths and promises is of very inferior moment. And this is the undeniable effect of Romish and Oxford theology. Every thing tends to aggrandize the sacramental functionary, and to disparage the preacher. A thorough Tractarian could never bring himself to write as the Apostle did in this Epistle. But St. Paul knew not this sacramental regeneration and justification, or knew it only to condemn its essential principles as they were advanced by the Judaizing teachers of his day. While he doubtless regarded every part of the Evangelic system, its rites, as well as its doctrines, with entire reverence, and rated each at its just point in the scale, he evidently judged his office as a preacher of the cross by far the most important entrusted to him, and in this he preëminently gloried. Not as a baptizer, but as a preacher of the unsearchable riches of Christ, he had begotten the Corinthians in the Gospel.

Romans 10 : 13, 14, implies the same truth. "For whosoever shall call upon the name of the Lord shall be saved. How then shall they call on Him in whom they have not believed? and how shall they believe in Him of whom they have not heard? and how shall they hear without a preacher?"

There the steps in the way of life are recounted, and conjoined—Salvation with prayer, prayer with faith, faith with the preached word, the word with the ministry, the ministry with the mission.

The frequent warnings in the New Testament against the tendency to substitute formal compliances for genuine holiness have an important bearing on this question; for such warnings certainly imply that the grace is not inseparable from the sign. Gal. 5 : 6. "For in Christ Jesus neither circumcision availeth any thing, nor uncircumcision; but faith which worketh by love." Note particularly 1 Cor. 10 : 1–5, compared with verse 11, "and these things are writted for our admonition."

The whole congregation of Israel were baptized unto Moses in the cloud and the sea, ate the same spiritual (sacramental) meat, and drank the same spiritual drink; yet with many of them God was not pleased. How can this be an admonition to Christians, except as warning them that, in spite of participation in the ordinances of Christ, they may still be subject to divine displeasure, and also perish?

The allegation that the spiritual new birth is inseparable from baptism is also disproved: 1. By scriptural examples of persons regenerate without baptism; 2. By scriptural examples of persons unregenerate after baptism.

The penitent thief was undoubtedly regenerated, or he could not have entered Paradise. Cornelius must have been, before his baptism, a regenerate person. It is hard to believe that the Roman centurion, (Matt. 8 : 10,) whose faith exceeded all that the Saviour had found in Israel, or the pardoned weeper, (Luke 7 : 47,) or the Syro-Phœnician woman, were unregenerate persons.

Then, as a proof that every one born of water is not also born of the Spirit, we have the notorious example of Simon Magus, (Acts 8.)

There is a manifest, and I think insuperable difficulty, presented by the case of holy men who lived before the coming of Christ, to this theory of inseparable baptismal regeneration. How could they be saved without regeneration? As the language of John 3 : 3, 6, is without limitation or exception, those who deduce from it the necessary union of baptism and regeneration have no right to interpose any qualification of their own. Pious Israelites before the institution of Christian baptism, could not, on their theory, be regenerate, and, unless regenerate, we insist, they could not enter the kingdom of God. If it be answered that the like blessing was conveyed under the old dispensation in circumcision, then they must admit the perfect application to baptism of St. Paul's assertion respecting the inefficacy of circumcision without a new creation, and this admission is fatal to their theory. And they must farther explain why circumcised persons, if already regenerate, were baptized at all, for there is but one new birth. The assertion is positively made, in the Tract before referred to, (No. 171 N. Y. Tract Society,) that "Regeneration was delayed till the coming of Jesus Christ in the flesh." "There had never been *a birth* of the Spirit." "One great misconception on the subject of regeneration has been the supposing it a grace known to the sons of men before the Gospel dispensation." The servants of God under the old dispensation, then, were never made his children by spiritual regeneration. They entered the kingdom of God without being born again; "for many shall come from the east and from the west, and shall sit down with Abraham, Isaac, and Jacob, in the kingdom of heaven."* Thus we are brought to a downright contradiction of our Saviour's words in John 3 : 3, "Except a man be born again, he can not see the kingdom of God."

The Scriptures make the fruits of the Spirit the only infallible sign of spiritual regeneration.

Gal. 5 : 22–25; 1 John, throughout.

Matt. 7 : 17–20.

"In this the children of God are manifest, and the

* Matt. 8 : 11.

children of the devil—whosoever doeth not righteousness is not of God." 1 John 3 : 10.

1 Peter 3 : 21, is a positive assertion that the baptism which saves us is not the external rite, but "the answer of a good conscience towards God." The baptized person, therefore, who is really advantaged by the rite, is one who is able, with a good conscience, to make the profession of repentance and faith, and the promise of obedience which are then required. But in order to do this sincerely, he must be already "transformed by the renewing of the mind," his understanding enlightened, his will brought into submission to the will of God, and his desires enkindled after holiness and heaven. It would seem as if, in this passage, the Holy Spirit designed to rebuke the very error which became in later ages so prevalent and pernicious, the substitution of the form of godliness for the power. The advocate of baptismal regeneration reads the beginning of this passage with joy and triumph. "Baptism doth also now save us." This is just his theory. But hold! St. Peter has not finished the sentence—"Not the putting away the filth of the flesh, but the answer of a good conscience towards God." Not the outward ablution, but the sincerity of the profession, the spiritual disposition, the new and contrite heart, willingly yielding itself to the service of God.

This denial is a death-blow to his theory. For the outward washing includes, he has maintained, the internal change and the complete blessing.

II. THE THEORY OF INSEPARABLE BAPTISMAL GRACE TESTED BY OBSERVATION AND EXPERIENCE.

Against this test its advocates strongly object. With them it is reckoned commendable faith to reject all such appeals. The more opposed their theory is to what we witness, to the testimony of our senses, the more room, according to them, for the exercise of faith. In this, as in some other points, there is a marked resemblance between them and the supporters of the dogma of transubstantiation. In either case, we are urged with the duty of unquestioning, implicit belief, and are warned against the presumption of attempting curiously to pry into the operations of God's Spirit.

But the distinction we must maintain to be clear and marked between the humble, reverent submission of faith *to what God has revealed*, and the prostration of the intellect in blind credulity *to what man has superadded.* The demands of the Scripture upon our faith are perfectly consistent with the exercise of our judgments, and the evidence of our senses. The service to which God calls us is truly a "reasonable service." There are doctrines, indeed, which exceed the capacity of the human, perhaps of the angelic intellect to grasp and fathom, which, being sufficiently attested as parts of a Divine revelation, it is our bounden duty to receive without cavil or doubt. These doctrines are not against reason, but above it. But matters of fact may be within the cognizance of those faculties wherewith God hath endowed us. And in regard to them, experience is never at variance with Scripture. Our Lord and his Apostles did not require men to believe in their miracles barely upon their word, but placed them before their senses, so that they could satisfy themselves of their reality. And truths of his religion meant to have practical influence, are never at variance with the testimony of experience. Christ calls himself "the light of the world"; and we find it an undeniable fact that those parts of the world in which his Gospel is known and received in its purity, are, as to their intellectual, moral, and religious state, in light, compared with other portions of the globe. He foretold, in the parable of the Sower, the different reception of his word by different classes of hearers; in that of the tares in the field, the mixed condition of his *visible* Church: and past history and the actual reality abundantly confirm the predictions. Let the distinction be carefully noted between doctrine and existing fact, and it will greatly help to disembarrass this subject. Doctrine really contained in Scripture we are bound to receive in humble, unquestioning faith. Alleged fact we may examine and inquire into; and if such it be, fair, candid, and searching inquiry will confirm and establish it. That all men are by nature corrupt and fallen, is at once a revealed doctrine and ascertainable fact. And the more closely the fact is examined into, the more clearly is the doctrine vindicated. But if the Bible should affirm that the skin of the Ethiopian was white, and that of the European black, here would be a statement not of religious doctrine but of fact, and when it was found contrary to the evidence of our senses, and to the common experience of mankind, with all our reverence for Scripture, we could not believe it. We could not, however reluctantly, but admit the testimony of our senses. Now, facts in morals are not as palpable to sense as in physics, but they are just as real, and as capable of ascertainment by the appropriate means. And the Scriptures, so far from discouraging, constantly appeal to this proof. To shut our eyes to such evidence, may expose us to be led blindfold in the path of error, or render us blind leaders of the blind, but is no proof of reverence or faith. Our Lord, for instance, warns his disciples, "Beware of false prophets, which come to you in sheep's clothing, but inwardly they are ravening wolves. Ye shall know them by their fruits. Do men gather grapes of thorns, or figs of thistles?" Here our Saviour directs his people to exercise their own observation and discernment respecting religious teachers. And he gives them a test whereby to discriminate between the faithful and trust-worthy guide and the plausible hypocrite; a test which he pronounces reliable and sufficient. Now, if a man surrender his reason and judgment to his spiritual guide, and refuse to examine into the truth of his pretensions by the test to which Christ hath directed, on the plea of exceeding reverence for the sacred office, and distrust of his own judgment, is his conduct that of reverential faith, or of superstitious credulity? Is it any mark of honor for the clergy to decline subjecting them to the test which the Saviour required? Close scrutiny may strip the sheep's clothing from the wolf, but it will only increase the claims of the upright and faithful to confidence and affection. Truth will always abide the test of examination, as gold comes out the purer and brighter from the furnace.

Now, the alleged new creation of the soul of every baptized infant, if it be so, is a fact, and a fact not rare and occasional, but very frequent; and a fact not far removed from our observation, but taking place under our very eyes. On the theory which we are considering, the fault and corruption of our nature, the seminal principle of all the wickedness that is in the world, is eradicated, or a new and more powerful principle of holiness is implanted. If such be indeed the case, we may expect to see the change exemplified in the tempers, dispositions, and conduct of baptized children. We may look for a marked contrast between children who have been and who have not been brought to the baptismal font. If the latter are self-willed, stubborn, froward, undutiful, averse to salutary restraint, to holy duties, to religious instructions, we may yet expect to see the former docile and amiable, pure and dutiful, averse from evil and inclined to good, manifesting an early interest in heavenly things, and cherishing childlike confidence and love toward their heavenly Father. In their case we may anticipate that the religious instructions imparted to them will be eagerly welcomed and truly followed. As their minds unfold, and they grow in stature and knowledge, we may look to see them growing in grace, and in favor with God and man. There are undeniable instances of children manifesting pious dispositions at a very early age. If all baptized children are temples of the Holy Ghost, as we are assured,* then we may reasonably look for such evidences of the Spirit's presence and power. For we have our Saviour's express word for it: "Make the tree good and his fruit will be good, for the tree is known by his fruit." But according to the advocate for Baptismal Regeneration, in the modern sense, the corrupt tree of our human nature is made good invariably, (in the case of infants,) at the baptismal font. If this be so, our Lord being witness, it will produce good fruit. "That which is born of the Spirit is spirit." The fruits of the Spirit are plainly described in Holy Writ. Gal. 5 : 22–24.

If the theory be correct, therefore, we shall have the grateful evidence thereof before us. In our households, our schools, our churches, we shall have the delightful task of training up holy children in the nurture and admonition of the Lord. The difference between a family baptized, and one unbaptized, will be like that between an Israelitish and an Egyptian dwelling, when Egypt was smitten with the ninth plague. Parents, teachers, and pastors

* "Born carnal, he has now a spiritual constitution, with spiritual faculties, faculties which he could never have inherited by his first birth, and whereby he can apprehend heavenly truth, and discern, obey, and love the spiritual law." "This covenanted presence of the Spirit in each baptized man is the only presence of the Spirit of which we at all know in any man." Tract No. 171, pp. 14, 15.

will have constant opportunities of realizing the happy and holy effects of Divine grace. And the country where all are brought to the healing waters, the abode of a nation of regenerate souls, will almost correspond with the bright prophetic delineations of that period, when "the knowledge of the Lord shall cover the earth as the waters cover the sea."

Such expectations I maintain to be not extravagant or unwarranted, but such as we might reasonably indulge from the Scriptural delineations of the great change which the Holy Spirit effects in its subject. "The fruit of the Spirit is in all goodness, and righteousness, and truth." "The new man, after God, is created in righteousness and true holiness." One of the chief causes of imperfect religion among regenerate adults is the previous growth of evil habits that have become fixed and inveterate with years. But this unfortunate fruit and effect of a corrupt nature, if the theory we are considering be founded in truth, will have been obviated and escaped by infant regeneration.

But we are answered that grace may be lost; that there are cases of adults baptized upon their own apparently sincere profession, who fall away; that there is a neglect on the part of parents, etc., to cherish the implanted baptismal germ, and that "the infection of our fallen nature doth remain, even in the regenerate."

I am not disposed here to controvert the position that grace may be irrecoverably lost, while, at the same time, there is great reason for thinking that our

Baptismal Service was framed by those who were of a different opinion. But, in a world of sin and temptation, we have sad and frequent cases of deplorable falls of those who once seemed to run well; and whether they ever recover themselves or not, is beyond our knowledge. Since we can not pronounce with infallible certainty, in our own case or another's, whether we be really new creatures in Christ, or whether, if we fall away, we shall ever be renewed again unto repentance, it is our wisdom to fear and deprecate any approach to declension and apostacy. But are we to believe that, in the dispensation of the Spirit, apostacy is the rule, and perseverance in grace the exception? Of our baptized youth, how large is the proportion who grow up from the cradle, "blameless and harmless, the sons of God, without rebuke, shining in the midst of a crooked and perverse generation, as lights in the world?" Baptismal grace ought to show itself in early godliness. Examples we occasionally meet with of children, who, from the first developments of reason, give indications of unfeigned piety. There is no impossibility in such manifestations of youthful religion. Why are they so rare? They ought to be the vast majority of those dedicated to the Lord in his ordinance, particularly where the parents are pious, perhaps priests and baptizers. Conversion, even in youth, is not the evidence which we require. The godly parent, who has no belief whatever in the invariable regeneration of baptized children, labors with and prays for his baptized offspring, reminds them of their solemn introduction into God's covenant, and pleads before God that transaction, and his promise to be a God not only to his people, but unto their children, and he receives at length a gracious answer in the conversion of his offspring. But the change, even in the youthful heart, is discoverable, the change from selfishness, indifference, and aversion to holy duties, to penitence, faith, and love. That change the parent can not doubt is from above; he may count it an answer to the prayers offered at the baptismal dedication of his child to God, as well as continually since; but he is fully persuaded that it did not take place in baptism, but years after. A period more or less extended, of folly and unholiness, intervened between the baptism of the child, and his experience of the Spirit's power. I do most devoutly believe that Infant Baptism, rightly appreciated, and followed by that assiduous care and instruction which are promised by parents and sponsors, will ordinarily issue in youthful piety, and that it is one great means, under the blessing of God, of bringing our youth to the early knowledge and acceptance of the Saviour's grace. But I am equally persuaded that this most desirable object will be hindered rather than promoted by unscriptural, exaggerated, and unreal exhibitions of the sacrament. Similar means may be employed by parents holding these widely different views of baptism. But in the one case, the child will be taught the necessity to his salvation of a thorough and radical change, and be encouraged to seek it from the Holy One, into whose covenant he hath been introduced, and be made to feel himself guilty and endangered until his heart be given to God. In the other case, he will be naturally led to flatter himself that all is well, and exhortations to improve his baptismal grace will be comparatively cold and pointless.

The fact is not to be denied, even by the most strenuous maintainers of Baptismal Regeneration, that the large majority of those baptized in infancy do not give any evidences of piety in childhood and youth.* But it is said, they were indeed spiritually changed, but the grace which they then received has been lost or forfeited. The seed of grace is so insecurely deposited, on this theory, that, as a general thing, it is speedily lost. But the Scripture not only declares, "Whosoever is born of God sinneth not," but moreover adds, "For his seed remaineth in him, and he can not sin, because he is born of God."† So

* "Blessed are they who cherish and improve their baptismal grace, and by fulfilling their baptismal vows, preserve inviolate their title, through the mercy of God in Jesus Christ, to their baptismal privileges. But, alas! this is not the case with the bulk of those who were baptized in infancy. They have neglected their baptismal vows, and forfeited their baptismal privileges."—*Bishop Hobart's Works*, ii. 489.

"Why is it that so many who, in baptism, were made the children of light, live as the children of darkness? Why is it that so many who, in baptism, were made the heirs of glory, live as if their portion was a perishing world? Why is it that so many who were marked in baptism as the soldiers and servants of Jesus Christ, forsake this Divine leader for the ranks of that rebellious host which the great Adversary is leading to perdition?"—*Ibid*, ii. 501.

† 1 John 3: 9.

that the "incorruptible seed," introduced by spiritual regeneration, is not so weak and perishable a thing, so easily up-rooted and withered. If we admit that it may be utterly lost by long resistance of the Spirit, we can not, in the face of this plain declaration, believe that it is ordinarily inefficacious and unfruitful.

The seed withers, we are told, because there is no subsequent care and nurture. The baptized child resists the holy tendency, and refuses to be led by the indwelling Spirit. But is not one most important office of the Holy Spirit the changing and sanctifying of *the will?* Thus, doth not God "order our unruly wills and affections," that "we may love the thing which He commands, and desire that which he does promise"? Doth not his grace prevent us "*that we may have a good will,*" as well as "work with us when we have it?" We require, as an evidence that baptized children are spiritually and morally regenerate, the fruits of the Spirit. It is answered, they have not been willing to cherish the holy principle imparted to them at baptism. They were disinclined to godliness. Aye, and why were they so disinclined? Because "that which is born of the flesh is flesh," and they are still "in the flesh." Had they been new created by the Spirit, they would have been willing to serve God and follow after holiness; for one effect of the blessed Spirit is to change and subdue the perverse will.*

* See Collect in the "Order of Confirmation."

Observe, further, that before children arrive at an age to be influenced by instruction or example, they give evidences of a fallen nature. Evil passions, such as anger, jealousy, envy, covetousness, and stubbornness betray themselves in the infantile conduct. Ought there not to be a palpable contrast between the tempers and dispositions of the new-born heirs of heaven, and of those who are yet "children of wrath"? These rising passions and unholy tempers were not imbibed from companions or pernicious examples. They are innate. They are evidences of the real nature, as much as the claws of the tiger's cub. And yet we are expected to believe that this nature is now altogether changed, and is like unto that of Adam before the Fall.

To evil examples and corrupting influences is traced the want of holy dispositions and conduct in so many of our baptized youth. But to what shall we ascribe the tendency on their part to follow evil examples, and yield to corrupting influences? Why are such children so much more easily drawn to what is evil than to what is good? Is it not the depravity of our fallen nature that is so powerful an auxiliary to what is pernicious, and such an obstacle to what is holy? But could this be so, if that depravity had been overcome by the regenerating Spirit? Would there not be manifested, in those healed of the hereditary plague of sin, a strength of holy principle that would not yield so readily to the assault of temptation?

It is one of the characteristics of creative wisdom

that its products are adapted to the condition and circumstances into which they are to be introduced. The animal and the plant are suited to the climate, the means of subsistence, the soil, and other influences to which they will be subjected. God forms them not in vain, nor launches them out into the world devoid of hardihood, endurance, and aptness to their lot. But what works of God are so precious in his sight as regenerate souls, on which his own holy image hath been restamped? And yet they are ushered into a world of temptation and sin, on this theory, with so much feebleness, imperfection, and inability to resist the poison circulating around them, that they die ere they can be ascertained to live. Surely, such a hypothesis is most incongruous with the infinite wisdom and goodness of the Almighty. If the analogy of the natural birth be urged as a reason why we may not expect that all should survive, surely the same analogy might lead us to the conviction that the larger portion should withstand the dangers to which they are exposed, and brightly evidence their heavenly birth. And when to this reasonable deduction from the works of God is added his own explicit declaration that the Divine "seed *remaineth* in him that is born of God," so that he can not be a willful and habitual sinner, that expectation is strengthened into confidence.

The original infection of our fallen nature doth remain indeed in the regenerate, but it remains not as the controlling principle in their hearts. A new and more powerful principle is at work there. "Sin shall not have dominion over you: for ye are not under the law, but under grace."* And where the whole temper and conduct breathe that carnal mind, which is enmity against God, how can we really believe that corrupt principle to have been subdued and transformed.

The advocates for the moral regeneration of all baptized infants often impute the absence of those effects which ought to result from it to the prevalent unbelief on this subject. Baptized children do not grow up pure and holy, because they are not explicitly taught that they are God's regenerate children. They are considered, and taught to consider themselves, as destitute of this new birth, and thus it is supposed the aspirations of their souls after God and holiness are discouraged and chilled, and they live according to the lower standard of unsanctified nature. But if a new heart were really given them in baptism, would it not so early manifest itself as to convince and persuade the most skeptical? The strong native bias of the child will make itself perceived and felt. There is an exceeding variety in the tastes, dispositions, capacities, and talents of the young. Parental influence may be exerted to encourage or repress the peculiar tendency, but the parent can not well be ignorant of it. Now, if the cast and bias of the mind show itself in every other respect, whether it be encouraged by the parent or not, how happens it that there is no manifestation of

* Rom. 6: 14.

the new and divine nature implanted by the Holy Ghost? Surely, this ought to be the most obvious of all qualities of the unfolding mind. The lovely and attractive traits of youthful piety should expand under the gentle breathings of the Spirit, like the flowers of spring when the south wind blows softly. And the most worldly-hearted or indifferent parent should be constrained to notice the fair promise and pleasant growth. Neither will unbelief, ridicule, or opposition prevent the appearance of these spiritual blossoms. Instances are not unknown of the development of early piety in the most unfriendly circumstances, such as to show us the vigor of the genuine plant, and lead us, where no such flower or fruit appears, to question the existence of the plant itself.

If the common incredulity on the subject of Baptismal Regeneration be the cause why its evidences are nipped in the bud, or presume not to bud at all, we may expect to find, where no such unbelief exists, a full and happy development of its results. The dogma of Baptismal Regeneration is undoubtedly held with the fullest confidence by the Romish Church, and the baptism of children is universal. In Italy, and Spain, and Mexico, no Protestant doubts or cavils prevent their full exhibition of the fruits of this system. If the incredulity of parents and friends extinguish the heavenly spark in countries professing the doctrines of the Reformation, we may look in Papal regions for the happiest evidences of its truth. The children are not only all regenerate in baptism, but they are taught themselves to believe it. No incredulity on this subject disturbs their minds. They are not called to the painful and troublesome task of searching for the fruits of the Spirit in their hearts and lives. Does the moral condition of these countries strengthen much the argument of the advocate for Baptismal Regeneration? Are the fruits of holiness there so manifest and abundant, that the observer is constrained to say, "God is with you of a truth"? Do not the prevailing vices, the moral darkness of lands over which is cast the shadow of the Papacy, witness with an overwhelming testimony, that the animating spirit is not the Holy Spirit of God? And yet how can this be, if the inhabitants, with scarce an exception, have all been new-born in the laver of regeneration, and acquiesce with the most implicit and unquestioning faith in this consolatory impression? The palpable moral inferiority of regions degraded by Romish superstition is unaccountable, on the theory of Baptismal Regeneration. Either the theory is false, or the regeneration thus conferred is valueless and inefficacious. It is a most unwarrantable disparagement and contempt of God's gifts, to make that, in its practical effects and issues, so worthless and unavailing, which his word represents as so unspeakably precious. Are we, indeed, required to believe that these hordes of the dissolute, vicious, and profane, are the sons of God by spiritual regeneration? Are these masses of the frivolous and the false, the deceitful and the unchaste, the multitude of deluded image and demon-worshippers, and their crafty and blind guides, all "partakers of the Divine nature"? Have they been "born again, not of corruptible seed, but of incorruptible," and "translated from the kingdom of darkness into that of God's dear Son"? I do not see why one who can accredit this, need hesitate at transubstantiation, or any of the miracles recorded in the legends of the Church of Rome. Yet there seems to me no escape from this consequence of the system. All baptized infants are regenerate, *ipso facto*, we are assured. But in Papal countries, all children are baptized. The vast numbers of illegitimate infants born therein are not allowed to want the sacrament. Neither is doubt suffered to prevent the full operation of grace received. But when we seek the manifestations of this grace, what do we find? St. John tells us, "He that committeth sin is of the devil." "Whosoever is born of God doth not commit sin. In this the children of God are manifest, and the children of the devil." Shall we believe with the Tractarian, that these workers of iniquity are the children of God, or, with St. John, that they are the children of the devil? Or if it be said that there is or may be some vicious element in Romanism (to kill in the bud the grace universally received in baptism) which does not exist in our Church; is it found that the children nurtured in those parts of our Church which are freest from unbelief in baptismal regeneration, decidedly exhibit a greater amount of the fruits of the Spirit?

The theory of inseparable baptismal regeneration doos not abide the test of facts. It is contradicted by experience. There is no such product of the fruits of holiness as we are warranted to expect. We demand as evidence the legitimate and necessary effects of Divine grace, the fruits of the Spirit. And we do not find them. That baptized youth, who are trained by those who know the truth as it is in Jesus, in the nurture and admonition of the Lord, will ordinarily manifest the happy and beautiful influence of early piety, is indeed a truth to which we fondly and trustingly cling. In such case, the covenant relation is followed by the performance of those duties of religious nurture, vigilance, and prayer, which it properly exacts. And in such cases the Divine blessing will not be withheld. God will bless his truth, presented by godly parents, sponsors, and pastors to the youthful mind, and render it effectual to the renewal of the soul in righteousness. Christian education is one of the most precious and powerful of all instrumentalities, and infant baptism is intended to impress upon those who have the care of youth, the importance of the duty. The devout and conscientious parent will be encouraged and stimulated, by the dedication of his offspring to the Lord, to the faithful use of the appointed means. In the morning he will sow his seed. By example and instruction, by shielding the young from pernicious associations, and placing them under holy influences, by line upon line, and precept upon precept, he will endeavor to train them in the way that they should go. And through the help of God, the labor will not be in vain, nor the prayer unanswered. The baptized youth who give evidences of piety, are, with very few exceptions, religiously-educated youth. And to attribute the renewal of such unto holiness to grace imparted at the moment of baptism, overlooking the important element of Christian nurture, and the promised blessing of God thereupon, is unwarrantable assumption. The advocate for inseparable baptismal grace maintains that all baptized children are spiritually regenerate. The more moderate defender of the practice of infant baptism, while not questioning what God may see fit to do in his unsearchable wisdom, finds spiritual regeneration ascribed in the Scriptures to the truth of God as its instrument, and looks believingly for the Divine blessing upon Christian nurture. As a matter of experience, neglected youth, although baptized, grow up in sin. Religiously-instructed youth grow up in the fear of God. And of this there are not infrequent instances, even among the unbaptized. On which side is the evidence of facts? And be it remembered, just theory as well as sound theology is never at irreconcilable war with realities.

III. The Tractarian Theory tested by the Standards of the Protestant Episcopal Church.

But we must proceed to the third test to which the theory under consideration was to be brought—namely, the standards of the Protestant Episcopal Church. And here the advocate of that theory fancies himself in his strongest ground, and gladly turns from unfavorable texts of Scripture, and unyielding facts, to what he considers his citadel, the Baptismal Service. This whole towering structure, indeed, of sacramental theology, rests upon a few liturgical expressions; a base most narrow and insecure for so prodigious an edifice. These expressions, especially the declaration in the Baptismal Service, "Seeing now, that this child is regenerate and grafted into the body of Christ's Church, let us give thanks," etc., are brought forward with an air of triumph, on every occasion, as if conclusive and unanswerable. That they are greatly misinterpreted and abused, will, I think, be evident to the candid inquirer into the whole scope and spirit of the Church formularies, and into the views and doctrines of the men by whom those formularies were compiled. The use made of this phraseology by the advocate of the system is strikingly similar to that made by the Roman controversialist, in the defense of transubstantiation, of our Saviour's words—"*This is my body.*" There is a constant repetition of the one phrase, and a claim that the words must be taken in the narrowest literal sense, irrespective of arguments from Scripture and reason. Indeed, the argument for the Romish view of the Eucharist, from the literal interpretation, is far stronger than that for inseparable baptismal Regeneration from the expressions in the Baptismal Office. The words of our Saviour, in the institution of the Supper, are not less plain and definite than the expressions of the Liturgy. If the literal sense of an isolated passage be of necessity the true one, then there can be no sufficient answer to the Romish theologian. Certainly, the words of Christ are not entitled to less reverence than a human composition. Let those who build so confidently upon the occurrence of this expression in the Baptismal Service, and denounce as unsound and dishonest their brethren, who can not subscribe to the interpretations put upon it by Bishop Philpotts and others of his school, enquire whether all their artillery can not be seized and turned upon themselves by their Romish adversary.

In the enquiry as to the doctrine of the Protestant Episcopal Church on the point before us, we naturally turn, first, to *the Articles of Religion.* In them we have the precise definitions, the authentic evidence of what the Church holds upon the subjects embraced therein. We decidedly maintain that for the ascertainment of her doctrinal views, the Articles are preëminently the standard of appeal. To know what the Church teaches upon a controverted subject, shall we not first recur to those formularies in which she professes to teach—wherein she defines her faith and proposes it to the acceptance of all who would seek at her altar permission to minister in holy things? If there be any difficulty in harmonizing different portions of her formularies, to which shall we attribute the chiefest weight and importance—to the fervent utterances occurring in a devotional office, or to the studied, unimpassioned, and guarded language of an Article, designed to embody and exhibit her belief, and produce consent among her children? Do we not reasonably expect in the latter a precision and perspicuity, a care and judgment in the selection of terms, for which in the former there is no necessity. The Church on her knees before the mercy-seat, or pouring forth her praises and thanksgivings to God, is not presumed to be so much occupied with niceties of language, as when she sits in Moses' seat, and authoritatively announces the truths and doctrines of her faith. To know what the Church teaches, must our attention be concentrated on her professed teaching, or on her prayers and praises? It might seem superfluous to insist upon so plain a point, but as a matter of fact we find the advocates for inseparable baptismal grace, endeavoring to make the baptismal office the chief or sole arbiter of the question in dispute. There they claim to find the key to the doctrine of the Church. Interpreting certain expressions therein occurring in the most unqualified and unlimited sense, they would make every thing else give way to this interpretation. If the Articles appear to teach differently, then the Articles must be conformed to this explanation, or must be left out of view.*

* As an illustration of the little regard paid to the dogmatic teaching of the Church in the Articles, it may be mentioned that in an elaborate discussion of this subject in the Church Review, (Art. II. July 1853,) in which the writer believes "that the great mass of Churchmen, who, unwedded to metaphysical speculations, are content to let Holy Scripture be its own interpreter, and who see in God's covenant in all ages and dispensations, more than an empty sign, etc., will say that the interpretation which we have presented is in harmony with God's word, with the whole system of the Church, with universal experience and observation, and with the greatest and best teachers in the Church,

Now, it is a claim founded upon the obvious principles of justice and reason, that, if there be a discrepancy between devotional and dogmatic standards, the greater weight in settling a controverted point, be given to the latter. For the very object of the latter is to speak the mind of the Church upon the subject in question. To ascertain the opinion of the Church upon the question whether original depravity be total or not, we should not concentrate our whole attention upon the confessions, and because the Church requires her worshippers, when bending low before the throne of a holy God, to affirm—"there is no health in us," thereupon consider the point as settled, without taking into consideration the 9th Article. The calendar appoints chapters from Apocryphal books to be read on certain days, and among the sentences to be read at the Offertory in the Communion Service, there are two from the same source. How shall we determine what degree of reverence the Church accords to the Apocrypha, and whether or not she reckons it as Canonical Scripture? Certainly by referring to Article VI., in which she precisely defines the Canon of Scripture, and from which we learn with what intent the Apocryphal portions, introduced into her services, are employed.

in every age;" in a discussion for which the writer anticipates such general and unqualified acquiescence, there is not a single allusion to the Articles on Baptism. The doctrine of the P. E. Church on this sacrament is supposed to be satisfactorily settled, and yet the very Article in which the Church defines her doctrine thereupon is unnoticed.

If, then, there did exist (which is by no means admitted) an evident opposition and contradiction between the language of the Baptismal Service and that of the Articles, it would be our duty to give the preference, in determining controverted points, to the latter. For, first, the very object and design of the Articles is to define, with clearness and precision, the doctrines of the Church. They constitute preëminently the symbol and standard, the definition and exposition, of her views. And, secondly, the Articles are of later date than the baptismal office, so that we are bound to consider that if there be any thing doubtful or obscure in the former, it is elucidated and explained by the latter. Coming after the liturgical forms, they must be considered as the mature and settled judgment of the Anglican Church upon the subjects therein embraced.

But it is far from us to attribute to the different portions of the Prayer-Book diversity and contradiction. We suppose them all capable of harmonious explanation. But we do maintain that the view of baptism, against which we here object, and which makes the sacrament to confer grace "*ex opere operato*" is contradictory to the sacramental Articles. We must do violence to the plain and definite teaching of the latter, if we acquiesce in the Tractarian interpretation of the former. In the ascertainment of the truth, we first examine the Articles, and determine what they fairly teach. Then we inquire whether the Baptismal Service admits of an interpretation consistent with the doctrine deduced from the

Articles, and such an interpretation presenting itself, we do not hesitate to receive it as satisfactory and true.

In Article XXV.—"Of the Sacraments," we first meet with the declaration, applied indifferently to both sacraments, that "in such only as worthily receive the same, have they a wholesome effect and operation." What is a worthy reception, is plainly set forth in the offices and the Catechism, namely, repentance and faith. So indispensable are these that before the Church allows baptism to be administered, they must be professed, personally, by the adult applicant, and through the mouth of sponsors by the infant.

"Baptism is not only a sign of profession, and mark of difference, whereby Christian men are discerned from others that be not christened, but it is also a sign of regeneration or new birth, whereby, as by an instrument, they that receive baptism rightly are grafted into the Church; the promises of the forgiveness of sin, and of our adoption to be the sons of God by the Holy Ghost, are visibly signed and sealed; Faith is confirmed, and Grace increased by virtue of prayer unto God."

"The baptism of young children is in any wise to be retained in the Church as most agreeable with the institution of Christ."

"Baptism is *a sign* of regeneration or new birth." But the difference is too plain for argument between the sign of a thing, and the thing itself. Yet the view against which we object confounds the sign and the thing signified. Baptism, according to the Tractarian theory, is not the sign of regeneration. It is regeneration. According to writers of that school, it is unscriptural and absurd to enforce upon baptized persons the necessity of being born again, or of testing the supposed fact of their regeneration by the fruits of the Spirit. If baptized, it is considered a matter of course, that they are regenerate and born again, not only of water, but of the Spirit. If such were the view of the Church, we should surely expect it to be declared in this explicit statement—"Baptism is regeneration" would have settled the matter. If it were left to the advocates of this theory at the present day to draw up an article on the subject of baptism, should we not have one of a very different tenor from Article XXVII?

"Baptism is a sign of regeneration, a symbol and outward representation of the new birth. Each sacrament is *verbum visible*, a sermon addressed to the eye—truth brought out in life and action before the senses. "Ye must be born again," is the emphatic language of the one. "Except ye eat the flesh of the Son of Man, and drink his blood, ye have no life in you," proclaims the other. In ordinary language, the sign and the thing signified may be used interchangeably, without confusion or erroneous impression. The Lord's Supper is commonly spoken of as "the Communion." Yet is there no communion of the body and blood of Christ therein to the unbelieving. For "the wicked, and such as be void of a lively faith, are in no wise partakers of Christ."

A portrait or a statue is the sign of the man, and may be called by his name, and yet there is no danger of misapprehension. The bended knee and the uplifted eye are the sign of devotion. But whether or not there is real prayer, the converse of a supplicating soul with God, is only known to the Searcher of hearts. When the Article testifies that Baptism is "a sign of regeneration," (*a sign*, the article indefinite, not *the sign*, the one exclusive inseparable index,) it uses language with the utmost precision, and furnishes a key to other passages in which the sign and the thing signified may be used interchangeably.* If the latter by themselves might lead to error or occasion perplexity, the former clear and accurate definition is at hand to obviate the doubt or danger.

"Whereby, as by an instrument, they that receive baptism rightly are grafted into the Church; the promises of the forgiveness of sin, and of our adoption to be the sons of God by the Holy Ghost, are visibly signed and sealed; faith is confirmed, and grace increased by virtue of prayer unto God."

If words are intended to convey meaning, this language makes evident the presumption of the Church that the applicant for baptism is a spiritually renewed person. To receive baptism "*rightly*" is to

* Thus in Article XV., "Of Christ alone without sin." "But all we the rest, although baptized and born again in Christ, yet offend in many things."

And Article XVI., "Of sin after Baptism." "After we have received the Holy Ghost, we may depart from grace given, and fall into sin."

receive it "truly repenting, and coming unto God by faith."* It is not affirmed that sins are then forgiven, and the baptized person then adopted as one of the sons of God. but that the promises of forgiveness and adoption are *then visibly signed and sealed.* To the already pardoned and adopted, the sign and seal of these inestimable blessings are in this solemn transaction openly extended. "Faith is *confirmed* and grace *increased*, by virtue of prayer unto God." But faith, to be confirmed, must be in previous existence, and grace, to be increased, must have been already enjoyed. What, then, is the condition before God of the applicant for baptism who truly corresponds with this representation? The word of God being the judge, he is spiritually regenerate, and "born again, not of corruptible seed, but of incorruptible." "Verily, verily, I say unto you, he that heareth my word, and believeth on Him that sent me, hath everlasting life, and shall not come into condemnation, *but is passed from death unto life.*"† "Therefore, being justified by faith, we have peace with God through our Lord Jesus Christ, by whom also we have access by faith into this grace wherein ye stand, and rejoice in hope of the glory of God."‡ "Whosoever believeth that Jesus is the Christ is born of God."§ And with this explicit, unambiguous testimony of the Divine word, the witness of the Protestant Episcopal Church is perfectly in accordance. The great truth that we are justified by faith only, is declared to be a most

* Office for baptism of adults.
† John 5: 24.
‡ Rom. 5: 1, 2.
§ 1 John 5: 1.

wholesome doctrine, and very full of comfort.* In "the declaration of Absolution, or Remission of Sins," in her stated service, she testifies that "God pardoneth and absolveth all those who truly repent, and unfeignedly believe his holy Gospel." And in the Homilies, we find "a true and constant faith," called "the root and well-spring of all newness of life."†

"The gift of faith" is testified to be "the first entry into the Christian life."‡ "Almighty God commonly worketh by means, and in this thing he hath also ordained a certain mean, whereby we may take fruit and profit to our soul's health. What mean is this? Forsooth, it is faith. Not an inconstant and wavering faith, but a sure, steadfast-grounded, and unfeigned faith. *God sent his Son into the world*, saith St. John. To what intent? *That whosoever believeth in him should not perish, but have life everlasting.* Mark these words, *That whosoever believeth in him.* Here is the mean whereby we must apply the fruits of Christ's death unto our deadly wound. Here is the mean whereby we must obtain eternal life, namely, Faith." "By this, then, you may well perceive that the only mean and instrument of salvation required of our parts is faith; that is to say, a sure trust and confidence in the mercies of God; whereby we persuade ourselves, that God both hath and will forgive our sins, that he hath accepted us

* Article XI.

† Page 405, second part of the Sermon concerning the Sacrament.

‡ Page 432, Homily for Rogation Week; third part.

again into his favor, that he hath released us from the bonds of damnation, and received us again into the number of his elect people, not for our merits or deserts, but only and solely for the merits of Christ's death and passion."* The penitent believer is justified before God. He is alive unto God. He hath passed from death unto life. He is pardoned and released from the condemnation of all his sins. He is born of God. All this is plain, incontrovertible deduction from the above-cited texts and quotations. Such was the conviction of the men who framed our standards, for the Homilies are their work. The great Scriptural doctrine, that the exercise of genuine faith is the transition from spiritual death to spiritual life, is confirmed by the most clear and energetic statements.

But on the theory that regeneration and baptism are inseparable, the penitent believer, before the sacrament is administered, is still unregenerate, unforgiven, not a child of God, but a child of wrath—an alien, still under condemnation. The new birth is, on either side, maintained to be the beginning of spiritual life. And if the candidate is baptized in order to his regeneration, he is, up to the moment of baptism, dead in trespasses and sins. Had the framers of our Articles and Homilies a particle of this theory in their minds? Was this startling proposition a part of their theology, that a true penitent, a sincere believer, one who can willingly renounce all sin, and yield himself to the service of God, is an unregene-

* Page 382, Second Sermon of the Passion.

rate person? Can a man exercise faith in Jesus, and yet be destitute of spiritual life? Can a man possess grace, and yet be unrenewed? But in Baptism, testifies the Church by this Article, "Faith is confirmed, and grace increased." Whence can a man derive penitence and faith but from the Spirit of God? And can the Spirit of God dwell in the soul, and there be no life there? So far, then, from the Sacramental system, which insists that spiritual life is communicated only through Baptism, being countenanced by the Article, its teaching is directly the reverse. It demands spiritual life as the preliminary to the sacrament. The sacramental seal is to be affixed only when all the assurance is had, which the imperfection of our mortal state admits, that the soul is already quickened and justified. Instead of the Church teaching that we become spiritually regenerate only in and by baptism, she teaches that to the spiritually regenerate alone is the privilege of baptism to be extended. They alone *receive baptism rightly.* They alone can render that "answer of a good conscience," wherewith the salutary effect of the sacrament is inseparably connected. Having already embraced in faith the promises of forgiveness and adoption, and having received through divine mercy, pardon and sonship, they are entitled to the visible signs and seals of these promises. Having received of God grace to repent and the gift of faith, they may look for this faith to be confirmed, and this grace increased in this impressive ordinance. Yet even this confirmation of faith and increase of grace is expected, not simply as the consequence of the ministration of the rite, but "by virtue of prayer unto God."

Such is the teaching of this article, plain, definite, and susceptible of proof by most certain warrants of Holy Writ. For in like manner do the Scriptures require the exercise of penitence and faith, as the preliminary to the right administration of baptism. "Repent and be baptized every one of you, in the name of Jesus Christ, for the remission of sins."* "See, here is water, what doth hinder me to be baptized? And Philip said, If thou believest with all thine heart, thou mayest."† "Then answered Peter, Can any man forbid water, that these should not be baptized which have received the Holy Ghost as well as we?"‡ With this plain testimony of Scripture the Article perfectly harmonizes.

The Article indeed has in view the baptism of adults. This necessarily arises from its close adherence to the Scripture, which is wholly silent respecting the effects of infant baptism, while it presents several instructive examples of the ministration of the rite to adults. Although we deduce arguments from various parts of Scripture in favor of the practice of baptizing infants, yet we find there no positive precept on the subject, and no express information as to the benefits therewith connected. And this silence is well worthy of note. The Scriptures are instructive, both in what they say, and in what they leave unsaid. They teach by omission, as well as

* Acts 2 : 38. † Acts 8 : 36, 37. ‡ Acts 10 : 47.

by express declaration. And in bringing the sacramental system, which rests upon the presumption that, after the Church is once established, her members, with very little exception, receive spiritual life in unconscious infancy at the baptismal font, to the test of Scripture, we might well be surprised to find that there is not a single text which contains this most important proposition. The base for this prodigious structure is altogether wanting. We are required to believe, under strong denunciations of unbelief and rationalism if we presume to doubt, that all baptized infants are new creatures in Christ Jesus. They are declared to be, without exception, the subjects of the most remarkable transformation of which the human soul is capable. And yet, when we search the Scriptures, with this theory in mind, we do not find a solitary text that conveys it, or even an express direction to baptize infants at all. Our Church imitates this cautious reserve of Scripture, and does not undertake to define farther than Scripture warrants. That rash dogmatism which grows most bold and positive where the Divine word is most reserved; which seeks to impose its own unfounded deductions as indubitable articles of faith, and which brands all who can not receive them as heretics and unbelievers, is not derived from her. Its parentage is too evidently to be sought in another, and very different communion.

The Article, therefore, in accordance with Scriptural example, when it would teach concerning baptism with preciseness and solidity, contemplates the case of adults. Adult baptism is the first and principal idea of baptism. It is baptism as presented in Apostolic practice. From this we must argue, and to this we must refer. In this we are to search for doctrine, and here we are to seek the key and explanation of all that pertains to the subject. And it is upon this principle that the Church has proceeded in the construction of her offices.

The Twenty-seventh Article does not overlook the case of infant baptism, but the notice given to it is very different from that which might be expected upon the sacramental theory. "The baptism of young children is in any wise to be retained in the Church, as most agreeable with the institution of Christ." Certainly this is not the language of a Church which attributes to the baptism of infants the certain infusion of a new nature, which considers it as the divine and sovereign remedy for the ruin of the Fall. On the sacramental theory, "the baptism of young children" is not merely "to be retained as most agreeable with the institution of Christ," but because it is the great means of healing the plague of sin, and of recovering lost and depraved beings to holiness. The young are to be brought to the life-giving waters, before they can oppose their own unruly wills to the reception of the grace imparted. They are, early and in advance of the power of temptation, to be transformed and new-created, that so they may grow up in holiness and meetness for heaven. Instead of looking to the Word of God and the various means of moral discipline for effecting the new birth, or trusting to the uncertain issue of baptism in riper years, when, peradventure, the want of proper qualifications may interpose an insurmountable hindrance to its salutary effects, all the most precious and desirable fruits of a death unto sin and a new birth unto righteousness are to be secured in infancy. Then, with comparative ease, and infallible certainty, the children of wrath are to be made the children of God, and that incorruptible seed is to be implanted which distinguishes the heirs of salvation from the heirs of hell. It can not be conceived that a Church which had such conceptions of the virtue of infant baptism, should make no allusion to them under such circumstances; much less in giving a reason for its observance, should employ language so tame and disparaging. Contrast the tone of this article with that employed by Tractarian writers upon the sacrament, and is not the difference most obvious and noteworthy? So far from dogmatizing upon the subject, from pronouncing positively upon the effects of infant baptism, from imposing her charitable hopes upon the consciences of men as doctrines of the faith, she is content with the modest assertion of the conformity of her practice "with the institution of Christ." She occupies no ground that is not tenable and firm, and is content to stand, humbly, but immovably, upon the word of God.

THE BAPTISMAL OFFICES.

THE teaching of the Articles being thus clear and definite, it is to be presumed that the Baptismal Offices are not contradictory thereto, their language being allowed "such just and favorable construction, as in common equity ought to be allowed to all human writings."* And if the offices are susceptible of two diverse interpretations, one of which harmonizes with, and the other is opposed to, the teaching of the Articles, we are required, on every principle of fair reasoning and equitable construction, to prefer the former. We can not suppose that what the Church declares and defines in one part of her formularies, she denies and subverts in another. We must believe that she intends to be consistent with herself, and that one system of doctrine pervades all her authoritative compositions. In ascertaining what this doctrine is, we are bound, for the plain and obvious reasons previously stated, to refer first to her own dogmatic expositions, her positive enactments, put forth for the very purpose of establishing her principles, wherein, of course, her expressions are most carefully studied and precisely worded. We look then to the Offices to ascertain whether, fairly interpreted, they admit of a sense harmonious with the plain import of the Articles. And this reasonable expectation is not disappointed.

We notice, in the outset, a close resemblance

* Preface to Prayer-Book.

between the two offices, that for the baptism of infants, and that intended for persons of riper years. There is the same preface, the same prayers, the same promises, and the same call to thanksgiving, with only such variation as is indispensable on account of the different ages of the subjects of baptism. The principal variation is in the Gospel appointed to be read, the exhortation following, and the post-baptismal prayers. The two services are constructed on a common principle, and we must infer, therefore, are subject to the same mode of interpretation. The office for adult baptism presents comparatively little difficulty. The qualifications required for the ordinance are sincere repentance and living faith. "Doubt ye not, therefore, but earnestly believe that he will favorably receive this present person, truly repenting and coming unto him by faith." The applicant is therefore, as has been shown, already spiritually regenerate. The Holy Spirit hath convinced of sin, led him to a heart-felt repentance, and willing renunciation thereof, and enabled him to look to the Lord Jesus Christ in prayer and faith. Thus he is born of God; he hath passed from death unto life. He has that quickening principle of faith which is called, in the Homilies, "the root and well-spring of life." Of this faith and penitence he now makes an open, unequivocal profession. He engages to renounce all iniquity, and to follow Jesus in a new and holy life. And thereupon he is, after the performance of the baptismal rite, pronounced regenerate. For now there is added to the belief of the heart, the profession of the mouth. The secret covenant between the penitent soul and the Saviour is now confirmed by the public covenant, the solemn transaction between the applicant for salvation and the Almighty Saviour. Until the man was thus openly grafted into the visible Church, the Church had no right to pronounce him a regenerate person. Whatever he might be in the sight of God, she could not recognize him as one of Christ's, until he made this good profession, and received the appointed sign and seal of his engrafting into Christ. The fact that prayer is previously offered that the candidate may be born again, and receive remission of his sins by spiritual regeneration, is no more a proof that God has not already bestowed these blessings, than the daily use of the Lord's Prayer, in which Christians supplicate for the forgiveness of their trespasses, is an evidence that none who use it are already forgiven. The Church is henceforth to know and consider him as a regenerate person, and what prayer more suitable, before the baptismal washing, than that he may be such in reality and truth? Unless we admit the unscriptural and unwarrantable idea that the true penitent, the sincere believer, the man willing to renounce the world, the flesh, and the devil, willing to take up his cross and follow Jesus, is still dead in trespasses and sins, we must believe that the blessing of pardon and adoption is already his. The inward and spiritual grace already received is the warrant for the Church to impart the outward visible sign. Let those who attach regeneration to the very moment of baptism, and deny that it is separable therefrom, tell us what is the spiritual state of a penitent believer, yet unbaptized. Is he still under the condemnation of his sins? Is he the child of wrath, and heir of perdition? Is he under the guidance of Satan, or of the Holy Ghost? Or do these emotions of contrition, fear of God, trust in Jesus, and abjuration of iniquity, spring spontaneously from his own heart? If so, the natural state of the heart is very different from that which Scripture represents. Instead of being "deceitful above all things, and desperately wicked," it is strongly inclined, in some men at least, to holiness and God. But if it be granted that the candidate who is in truth what the Church supposes, is "led by the Spirit," then he is already a "child of God." (Rom. 8 : 14.) And how a child of God, unless born again of the Spirit? The Romish Church, which does hold that sacraments confer grace, *ex opere operato*, which knows no other than baptismal regeneration, the real parent of this dogma of inseparable sacramental grace, is perfectly consistent with herself in not exacting the previous qualification of a living faith. She naturally and necessarily considers a dead faith to be all that is needed. Indeed, if spiritual life only come through this channel, it can be only a dead faith which precedes the rite. And if our own Church agreed with Rome in the doctrine, as the Bishop of Exeter affirmed, she would equally agree in the qualifications required for baptism.

To combine this Romish doctrine with our Articles

and Offices, we must confound the great and radical distinction between a dead faith and a living, since on this theory they may both equally exist in an unregenerate person. We must consider that penitence, faith, and the purpose of full obedience are not the fruits of the Spirit. And thus we must adopt rank Pelagianism, and believe that man is not by nature corrupt and very far gone from original righteousness, for a corrupt tree can not bring forth good fruit. And who can deny that the dispositions required of the applicant for baptism are good fruit? If it be contended that these are holy dispositions, and implanted by the Spirit in the soul, but that they are not the grace of regeneration, which is only conveyed in baptism, we reply that there is no scriptural warrant for any such distinction. We have yet to learn from the Bible how a man can exercise holy dispositions without being born again. There we find that the tree is known by its fruit—and that "the fruit of the Spirit is in all goodness and righteousness and truth." "That which is born of the flesh is flesh, and that which is born of the Spirit is Spirit." There we learn that they who "have purified their souls, by obeying the truth through the Spirit," are "born again, not of corruptible seed, but of incorruptible, by the word of God." "Whosoever believeth that Jesus is the Christ is born of God." This sophistical distinction can not bear the light of God's word. It is without Scripture, as it is without reason to support it. It confounds the marked opposition between sin and holiness, between the carnal and the spiritual mind, between the works of the flesh and the works of the Spirit, between nature and grace. According to this theory, all the prominent and lovely lineaments of the Christian character can exist and flourish without the new birth—and by parallel perversion of the truth, in the case of those baptized in infancy, all the sinful propensities and unholy dispositions of our nature can abide unchecked and dominant in the regenerate. Is not this like calling evil good, and good evil, putting darkness for light, and light for darkness: bitter for sweet, and sweet for bitter?

The Office for the baptism of adults fully sustains the view deduced from the Article that the applicant is supposed to be already spiritually regenerate. Such is the purport of his profession. That profession is presumed to be sincere. The Church gives it full credit, and thereupon, after imparting the appointed seal of the covenant, does not hesitate to pronounce the baptized person regenerate. The subsequent recognition of the regenerate state and character of the newly-baptized person, is founded upon the supposed sincerity of the profession. The Church can not construct offices of public worship on any other ground. Her worship and sacraments are not intended for hypocrites and self-deceivers, but for the believing and spiritually minded. If hypocrites and self-deceivers do intrude into them, they come unbidden and unblessed. They are warned against the presumptuous act, and taught to expect no benefit therefrom. (Art. XXV.) But it is evidently possible that such persons may come to Christian ordinances. Our Saviour, in several impressive parables, gives us reason to suppose that this will be the case. Persons will come to baptism, as Simon Magus did, devoid of the qualifications which God requires: what then? Are they regenerate? So far from it, that we have scriptural warrant for the assertion that they have "neither part nor lot in the matter," but remain after their baptism, still "in the gall of bitterness and bond of iniquity." And yet such persons were pronounced regenerate by the minister who baptized them. For it was not his prerogative to search the heart. The right profession was made to him, and he acted on the presumption of its truthfulness. Had he certainly known the unfitness of the applicant, it would have been his duty to reject him. Had he reason to suspect it, he would, as a faithful dispenser of the word and sacraments, have admonished, instructed and cautioned the applicant. But the appearance being fair, the judgment must be that of charity. And inasmuch as the necessary profession is made and the obligations of the Christian covenant are fully assumed, it is right and proper to declare the baptized person a partaker of its blessings. He knows, or if he does not, the minister is unfaithful to his trust, what manner of person he ought to be. And on the supposition that such he really is, he is pronounced regenerate. This declaration is therefore conditional. There is pre-supposed the spiritual fitness of the baptized person. Although absolute in its terms, it is hypothetical in reality. The connection is close and inseparable between the profession of faith before the baptism, and the declaration and thanksgiving thereafter. Any other view involves the strange, unscriptural, and absurd inference, that the hypocrite and the self-deceiver derive the same blessing from the sacrament, with the believing, penitent, and sincere.

THE OFFICE OF BAPTISM FOR INFANTS.

THIS office is, as has been remarked, almost identical with that provided for adults. The baptism is not administered until after the very same profession of penitence, faith, and obedience, as in the case of persons who have come to years of discretion. The solemn promise and vow is the same for each. Although, in the office for infant baptism, this profession is made by the mouth of sponsors, yet it is regarded as the act of the child. The infant and not the sponsor "renounces the devil and all his works, the vain pomp and glory of the world, with all covetous desires of the same, and the sinful desires of the flesh," and promises, "by God's help, not to follow nor be led by them." The infant, not the sponsor, "desires to be baptized in this faith"—for the sponsor is already a baptized person, and does not present himself for the sacrament. The infant, not the sponsor, promises "obediently to keep God's holy will and commandments, and to walk in the same through life." Thus the infant makes the very same profession which the adult makes which only the adult who is spiritually regenerate can make in sincerity and truth. After this profession, treating it as a reality, assuming its sincerity and truthfulness, just as in the case of adults, the infant is pronounced regenerate. And that, upon this profession, and this alone, is predicated the subsequent declaration and thanksgiving, is confirmed by the language of the Catechism.

Q. "What is required of persons to be baptized?

A. "Repentance, whereby they forsake sin; and faith, whereby they steadfastly believe the promises of God made to them in that sacrament.

Q. "Why then are infants baptized, when by reason of their tender age they can not perform them?

A. "Because they promise them both by their sureties; which promise, when they come to age, themselves are bound to perform."

Here, then, is the explanation given by the Church, of the grounds of infant baptism. If the Church held the Romish and Tractarian view of the spiritual regeneration, or new creation of all baptized infants, *ex opere operato*, how could she avoid giving that as the reason why they should be brought to the baptismal font? Their inability to exercise repentance and faith is no difficulty with the holders of this theory. It is enough, they tell us, that infants can not, by positive infidelity, oppose any obex or hindrance to the work of the regenerating Spirit. Their tender age, disqualifying them for acts of moral responsibility, instead of being an objection to ministering the ordinance, is on this supposition the very reason of all others why it should be then imparted. For while, in the case of adults, the efficacy of the ordinance is contingent and conditional, with unconscious babes it is supposed to be necessary and inevitable. The holder of this theory never, therefore, could ask such a question as the Church asks in this Catechism, or render such an answer. The believer in this theory, and the Church, look at the subject from a very different stand-point. For the very fact to which the Church refers, as possibly constituting a valid objection to infant baptism, is with the Tractarian its great argument and recommendation. And the Church is very far from giving any such reason for her usage as the Tractarian would give. She presumes nothing respecting the influence of the Holy Spirit upon the infant soul at the moment of baptism, because on that subject she knows nothing. The Scripture is silent, and she does not undertake to be wise above what is written. But she gives it as the explanation of infant baptism, that the child ostensibly enters into the covenant, by the agency of his sponsors, and incurs thereby solemn obligation to perform, at a subsequent period, the promises made in his behalf. We can not but notice, then, what weight and importance is attached in the Catechism to this part of the Baptismal Service. It is made the very ground of administering the sacrament. Infants may be baptized, as well as adults, because they make the same previous profession of repentance and faith. Now, we must insist that the subsequent language of the Office: "Seeing now, dearly beloved brethren, that this child is regenerate, and grafted into the body of Christ's Church, let us give thanks unto Almighty God for these benefits," etc., and the similar language of the thanksgiving, are to be taken *in connection with the previous profession*, just as in the case of adults. And we must insist that the same principle of interpretation be applied to the two parts of the service. It is doing violence to the laws of fair interpretation to apply an entirely different principle to different portions of the same instrument. If the former part can not be construed literally, and the attempt involves absurdity, it is unreasonable to impose the literal construction on the latter part. Yet this is the palpable and glaring inconsistency of the advocate of the necessary spiritual regeneration of all baptized infants. We must believe it, he argues, because the Church positively declares all baptized infants to be regenerate. Aye, but before this, does not the Church just as positively demand from these same infants a profession of faith, and a vow of obedience? Do not these very babes declare just as positively their renunciation of sin, and their desire to receive the sacrament? The sponsor is but the mouth-piece. The child is the actual party to the covenant. The repentance, faith, purpose of obedience, and desire for baptism, are those of the child, not of the sponsor. This, every one knows, is not a reality. But it is taken to be a reality. The Church treats it as such, and upon the strength of it proceeds to administer the Sacrament. Now, the Tractarian interprets these two portions of the service on entirely opposite principles. He understands the previous profession to be of the nature of a legal fiction—a transaction real indeed, and solemn in one view, but unreal and fictitious in another. For common-sense forbids him to suppose the infant of a few weeks old to be intelligently desirous of holy baptism. But if he be the child's sponsor, he declares this positively and unequivocally. He makes use of language to which he can not possibly attach the literal meaning. And then, a few minutes after, he seizes upon other language, occurring in the very same service, part and parcel of the identical transaction, connected with it intimately as consequent with antecedent, inference with premise, and he insists that this latter language shall be taken in the most strict and literal sense. He makes it expressive of absolute fact and indubitable reality, will hear not a word of hypothesis or explanation, and taxes all his brethren, who can not assent to the same assumption, with inconsistency and treachery. Nay, when he has the power, he is ready to drive away from the altars of the Church faithful and good men, who can not discard their convictions of the truth of God, or put upon the formularies of their Church a Romish interpretation which they were never meant to bear. Let the Tractarian apply to the complete service one explanation, either take the whole literally, or consent to such explanation as is fair and reasonable of all its parts. We deny his right to explain one portion as fictitious and hypothetical, and then fasten upon the other the most strict and unqualified literal sense. The demand to apply to the expression, touching the regeneration of the baptized infant, the same mode of explanation to which he is compelled to resort in the same service, is perfectly just and reasonable. We claim that the service be viewed as a whole, that the same laws of interpretation be applied to one part as to another; that no sweeping deductions be made from isolated expressions; that the two offices for adults and infants be compared together, and that particular weight be given to the article expressly designed to convey the doctrine of the Church on this very subject. Thus it is that we proceed in interpreting the Holy Scriptures. Isolate a text, separate it from the context, shut out all light from other parts of Scripture, and you may arrive at any conclusion you choose, except the truth. Thus the Romanist proves the supremacy of the Papacy from the words, "Thou art Peter, and upon this Rock I will build my Church," and judicial priestly absolution from John 20 : 23, and justification by works from James 2 : 24.

With no less force and plausibility does the Socinian argue from such a passage as John 14 : 28, "My Father is greater than I." In precisely the same way is the doctrine of Baptismal Regeneration, in the most extravagant sense, proved from the expressions in the post-Baptismal service; and this assumption being regarded as an axiom, the remainder of the Office, Articles, Homilies, Scripture, all must give way, and be bent and twisted into conformity with this foundation fallacy.

In the baptismal service for infants, as in that for adults, the covenant of salvation between God and man is brought out very distinctly and emphatically The conditions of that covenant on the part of man, and the blessings promised on the part of his Maker are presented, as well as the connection between the two. The intimate nature of this connection is shown by making the one a preliminary to the other. The Church will not consent to the administering of the rite, until after the profession and the promise of the conditions. She first demands evidence of the death unto sin and the new birth unto righteousness; then affixes the seal of the covenant, and returns thanks to God for the vouchsafement of his grace. Repentance and faith are judged by her so indispensable to the reception of the baptismal blessing, that the unconscious babe must profess them, before being washed with the sacramental water. When the condition is actualized, at a subsequent period, in the personal belief and penitence of the baptized child, then all the dependent benefits are rendered actual also. The transaction is like to the conveyance of an estate upon condition to an infant, the guardian engaging in the infant's name the prescribed conditions, but the actual vesting of the estate taking place when the conditions are actually performed. The Church indulges the charitable and confident expectation that these conditions will assuredly be performed. The language is that of elevated faith and charity. And she not only presumes, therefore, the regeneration of the baptized child, but his ultimate salvation. "Doubt ye not, therefore, but earnestly believe that he will likewise favorably receive this present infant; that he will embrace him with the arms of his mercy, that he will give unto him the blessing of eternal life, and make him partaker of his everlasting kingdom." So that the language of the Church is confident respecting the final salvation of the baptized infant, as well as his regeneration. And if we must understand the Office as teaching that all baptized infants are spiritually regenerate, I know not why we are not equally bound to gather therefrom that all baptized infants are finally saved.

THE CATECHISM.

The answer to the second question of the Catechism is nearly as much relied on by the advocate for inseparable baptismal regeneration as the Office for Infant Baptism. A fair and candid examination of the whole formulary will no more sustain these enormous inferences than in the case of the Baptismal Offices. It is important to observe, first, the state of mind expressed by the Catechumen. The Catechism is connected with the Office for Confirmation. It is entitled, "A catechism, that is to say, an Instruction to be learned by every person before he be brought to be confirmed by the Bishop." The spiritual qualifications of the candidate for Confirmation are the same with those required of the applicant for adult Baptism, and of the communicant. For

Confirmation is the door of entrance, the solemn and public admission to the privilege of the Lord's table.* Repentance and faith are demanded in each case, and are supposed to exist in the worthy participant in these rites. The Catechumen, in the view of the Church, is consequently a believing penitent, and therefore, in the highest and truest sense, a regenerate person. Such an one is certainly "a member of Christ, a child of God, and an inheritor of the kingdom of heaven," "born both of water and of the spirit. But inasmuch as Baptism was the Divine attestation of this covenant, when the promises of God were visibly signed and sealed, the early dedication to God in his blessed covenant, of one who now with a good conscience assumes its vow and obligations, there is a natural retrospect to that transaction. Connecting together the symbol and the grace now actually enjoined, the Catechumen looks back to his baptism as the occasion of imparting to him the seal of these precious benefits. And there is here presented, in that usual and inseparable union to which reference has been already made, the conditions of the covenant on the one hand, and its blessings on the other. The question immediately follows, "What did your Sponsors then for you?" And the answer recites the terms of the promise and vow—the penitent renunciation of sin, the profession of faith, and the promise of obedience. We have no more right to dissociate the two parts of the transaction in the Catechism, than in the Office.

* Rubrics after Offices for Adult Baptism and Confirmation.

In each case are exhibited to us conjointly, the promises and the conditions. They are inseparable. The conditions failing, the promises and blessings are made void. The conditions being made actual, the blessings are fully received and enjoyed. The Catechumen is supposed to be one in whose case the conditions are realized. Of this there is conclusive proof, as well in the readiness to receive the laying on of hands, as in the answer to the question—"Dost thou not think that thou art bound to believe and to do as they have promised for thee? *Answer*. Yes, verily; and by God's help so I will. And I heartily thank our Heavenly Father that he hath called me to this state of salvation, through Jesus Christ our Saviour. And I pray unto God to give me his grace, that I may continue in the same unto my life's end." Here is the heart believing unto righteousness, and the mouth making confession unto salvation. But suppose this answer to be utterly false, and that the Catechumen does not sincerely recognize the obligations assumed in his behalf by the Sponsors. Suppose that there is in reality no thankfulness to God for being called to a state of salvation, and no sincere prayer for his grace to enable the baptized child to continue therein. In such a case is the Catechumen a member of Christ, a child of God, and an inheritor of the Kingdom? Having come to an age to understand the nature of the transaction, having been taught what a solemn vow, promise, and profession has been made in his name, and profanely despising, like Esau, his birthright, may he apply to himself the holy titles and unspeakable privileges of sonship and reconciliation? Is not the disobedient, impenitent, ungrateful, prayerless youth in the gall of bitterness and in the bond of iniquity? And will he not continue, until brought to repentance, an enemy to Christ, a child of the devil and an heir of hell? If the Catechism, as is alleged, requires us to believe every baptized Catechumen regenerate, it equally requires us to believe him to be *sanctified.* "I learn to believe in the Holy Ghost, who sanctifieth me and all the people of God." The one is just as strongly affirmed as the other. The language there, as in the Baptismal Office, proves too much for the theory which is built upon it. The only consistent explanation is that which considers it as the utterance of a truly converted and accepted person, one actually exercising holy dispositions, and claiming with loving faith the blessings of the new covenant. This view harmonizes the whole language of the Catechism. The Catechumen was baptized in infancy, because repentance and faith, of which he was then incapable, were promised for him by his Sponsors; not that he might as a matter of course receive a new nature at the font. Arrived at an age to appreciate the mercies of God in Christ, he has felt, as a sinful being, his need of pardon, and has applied in penitence and faith to the Saviour of the soul. He recognizes, with devout gratitude, the distinguishing goodness of God in his early introduction into the visible Church, his dedication to the Redeemer through his own appointed ordinance, his access to Christian privileges, and his nurture under holy influences. And he presents himself, with a ready heart, to ratify and confirm the covenant of salvation. Hence he uses, and has a right to use, the language of appropriating faith, and lays hold upon the promises which were visibly signified and sealed to him at his baptism. Such is claimed to be a fair and reasonable interpretation of this formulary.

JUSTIFICATION BY FAITH.

THOSE who insist upon the universal application of the second answer to every baptized child, are bound to carry the principle through the whole. It must hold good as certainly of the subsequent answers. It will prove the holy disposition expressed in the fourth answer to pertain to all, and require us to believe that every baptized child is sanctified by the Holy Ghost, and is numbered among the people of God. It would seem difficult, after this, to question the salvation of all the Baptized.

The view of Baptismal Regeneration here opposed, can not be that of our Church, because it is wholly inconsistent with the doctrine of Justification by Faith. There is a palpable incongruity between the two. This is felt by many of the more consistent and thorough maintainers of the Sacramental theory, and hence their repugnance to Justification by faith is either openly manifested or very imperfectly concealed. Regeneration and Justification are not separable. A child of God, a partaker of the Divine nature, a new creature in Christ, can not be in a state of condemnation. Baptismal Regeneration necessarily draws after it Baptismal Justification.* But here the Sacramentarian comes into direct collision with our Church. If any thing is indubitable, it is her sanction of the doctrine of *Justification by Faith alone.* Her Articles declare and define it in the clearest and most emphatic terms. Her Homilies are full of it. Her Liturgy is pervaded with it. Her reformers suffered and bled for it. We must make our choice between the two principles. They are each master principles in theology. They give their coloring to the whole system of faith. They are utterly opposed in their practical tendencies. For pardon and peace with God, the one sends the sinner to the Saviour on his mediatorial throne, the other to the priest, at the font and the altar. The one assures the baptized that he hath already passed from death unto life. The other warns him, that if he be carnally minded, he is still in the flesh—that if he have never yet come to Jesus Christ in hearty repentance and true faith, there is no life in him; and in such case testifies unto him, that except he be born again, he can not see the kingdom of God. No sophistical comments, or labored ingenuity, can reconcile these two systems. The one was the key-note of the Reformation, was dear to the hearts, enshrined in the symbols,

* This is the consistent doctrine of Rome. "The instrumental cause of our justification is the sacrament of Baptism, which is the sacrament of Faith, without which no one ever obtained justification."—*Council of Trent*, Sess. vi. Cap. viii.

and sealed with the blood of its Martyrs. The other gave shape and coloring to the Tridentine system. We must choose between them. We can not fairly and permanently make them coalesce.

We leave the consideration of the standards of the Protestant Episcopal Church with a few brief quotations from the Homilies. He who undertakes to reconcile them with the theory, that all baptized persons are spiritually regenerate, may well be admired for his boldness.

"For it is the Holy Ghost, and no other thing, that doth quicken the minds of men, stirring up good and godly motions in their hearts, which are agreeable to the will and commandment of God, such as otherwise of their own crooked and perverse natures they should never have. *That which is born of the flesh*, saith Christ, *is flesh, and that which is born of the Spirit is Spirit.* As who should say, man of his own nature, is fleshly and carnal, corrupt and naught, sinful and disobedient to God, without any spark of goodness in him, without any virtuous or godly motion, only given to evil thoughts and wicked deeds. As for the works of the Spirit, the fruits of faith, charitable and godly motions, if he have any at all in him, they proceed only of the Holy Ghost, who is the only worker of our sanctification, and maketh us new men in Christ Jesus."

"Such is the power of the Holy Ghost to regenerate men, and as it were bring them forth anew, so that they shall be nothing like the men that they were before."

"Neither doth he think it sufficient inwardly to work the spiritual and new birth of man, unless he do also dwell and abide in him."

"Oh! but how shall I know that the Holy Ghost is within me? some man perchance will say. Forsooth, as the tree is known by his fruit, so also is the Holy Ghost. The fruits of the Holy Ghost, according to the mind of St. Paul, are these, (Gal. 5:22, 23.) Contrariwise the deeds of the flesh are these, (Gal. 5:19–21.) Here now is that glass wherein thou must behold thyself and discern whether thou hast the Holy Ghost within thee, or the spirit of the flesh. If thou see that thy works be virtuous and good, consonant to the prescript rule of God's word, savoring and tasting not of the flesh, but of the spirit, then assure thyself, that thou art endued with the Holy Ghost; otherwise, in thinking well of thyself, thou dost nothing else but deceive thyself."*

CONSEQUENCES.

THERE are consequences, it is conceived, necessary and unavoidable consequences of the dogma, that spiritual regeneration takes place invariably in infant baptism, and takes place in adults as well as infants, only in baptism, so revolting that they are enough to condemn it.

1. Whereas the Holy Scripture attributes the bestowment of spiritual life to the good pleasure and

* First part of the Sermon for Whitsunday.

sovereign will of the Holy Spirit, this theory subjects his most important operation under the Gospel dispensation to the will of man. If, as the sacramental theory asserts, the new birth is coincident with baptism, and may not take place except in baptism, then the new-creating energy of the Spirit is at the absolute disposal of man. The Infinite and Mighty God can not regenerate a soul until the priest perform the outward rite. And he must regenerate the soul of an infant whenever the priest shall see fit to baptize it with water.

Another consequence is the perdition of all the unbaptized. Regeneration is absolutely and universally necessary to salvation. "Except a man be born again, he can not see the Kingdom of God." "*Ye must be born again.*" The holy kingdom demands of all its inhabitants a new nature. And this nature is only attainable, on the theory we are considering, in Baptism. I have before adverted to the condition of those who lived under the old dispensation, and its virtual denial of hope to them. There would seem no escape to the holders of this opinion, from the universal condemnation of the Heathen world, infants as well as adults. And unbaptized infants who die in their childhood, in Christian lands, are subject to the same pitiless doom. This will be denied by the charitable and kindly, who yet adopt the theory from which it is a necessary deduction. But how can they deny it consistently with their interpretation of the 3d chapter of John? "If baptism and 'being born again' be terms of the same meaning, or if the one invariably accompanies the other, so that all who are rightly baptized are regenerate, and none else; then all who die unbaptized, even infants, as well as all others, all over the earth, and in every age of the world, without exception, are shut out of heaven! A proposition far more dreadful than any held by the most unfeeling and presumptuous Supralapsarian Calvinist."*

It will be hard, if not impossible, if this theory be correct, to vindicate our own Church from the charge of great inhumanity in imposing such restrictions as are found in her rubrics on the ministration of baptism to infants. How can she be justified in setting any limitations to so unspeakable a blessing? For every infant presented at the font, she requires three sponsors. And baptism must be administered in the Church, except in cases of real necessity. These requirements diminish very considerably the number of those who receive the sacrament. If the performance of the rite by the priest of course regenerates that infant, the greatest possible liberty and encouragement should be afforded thereto. So far from obstructing the work by exacting rubrics, let the regenerator be sent into the highways, and let him go from house to house, dispensing with open hand the inestimable gift of a new and holy nature. Let him not, on account of the objections of parents and guardians, hesitate to make their children new creatures in Christ, and inheritors of the kingdom of heaven. Why should he refrain from saving the infant's soul, because the parent is obstinate and unbelieving? Why should he not, like the Jesuit missionaries in China, sprinkle the crowds as he walks through the streets and market-places, with consecrated water, muttering the baptismal formula? Such a course, instead of being extravagant and absurd, would be the natural prompting of faith in this dogma. The unconscious infant can interpose no obex or hindrance. Go out, then, on your mission of love, and suffer not a babe to perish in its unblessed and unregenerate state! The requirements of our Church are reasonable and justifiable, if the rite be regarded as the dedication of the offspring of Christian parents to the Lord, in prayer and faith, to be trained up, by those who have presented them, in the way of holiness; an impressive introduction to a Christian education, wherefrom we look in due time for the Divine blessing. But on the supposition that the grace of regeneration is inseparable from the sacrament, any restrictions whatever are indefensible, inhuman, and unchristian.

The theory, therefore, that makes spiritual regeneration (a change not ecclesiastical, but internal and moral) inseparable from baptism, or at any rate, from infant baptism, is untenable. If the preceding reasoning be correct, it is shown:

1. Not to be the teaching of Scripture. Regeneration is thereby ascribed to the Holy Spirit as the Agent, and to the Word of God as the instrument, apprehended on our part by faith.

2. It is not confirmed by observation and experience, but is perpetually contradicted by them.

3. It is not the teaching of the Articles of Religion of the Protestant Episcopal Church.

4. It is not the sense of the Baptismal Offices, interpreted fairly as a whole, and in harmony with the Articles.

5. It is contradicted by the Homilies.

6. It is irreconcilable with the doctrine of Justification by Faith alone, which is undoubtedly held by our Church.

7. It draws with it consequences of an irreverent and revolting character, arrogating to man what is the sole prerogative of God, and making spiritual regeneration dependent on the will of man.

8. It leaves no hope for unbaptized infants, of whom hundreds are hourly passing into eternity.

9. It tends to produce very low and inadequate views of the nature of the change wrought by the Holy Spirit in our regeneration. In order to make doctrine agree with undeniable fact, it reduces the great spiritual transformation, the new-creation of the soul, to something undiscernable. The mass of frivolous, undevout, giddy, or profane youth, who have been baptized, are, on this theory, born again, made new creatures in Christ Jesus. They have experienced a death unto sin, and a new birth unto righteousness. They are not in the flesh, but in the Spirit. They have passed from death unto life; are turned from darkness to light; are partakers of the Divine nature; are temples of the Holy Ghost. But,

alas! how little in many cases do their tempers, dispositions, and lives correspond with this elevated description! There is nothing to distinguish them from the ungodly and unbelieving world, except this one thing.*

Either the theory of baptismal regeneration must be given up, or the standard of a regenerate state must be exceedingly lowered. Christian holiness must be brought down to the level of worldly or less than worldly morality, with the superaddition of compliance with the rites of the Church. The spiritual mind, the tender conscience, the sensitive dread of sin, the longing for the light of God's countenance, the affections set on things above, the hungering and thirsting after righteousness, the joy and peace in believing, the glowing expansive charity —all the lovely lineaments of the new creature in Christ Jesus will be disparaged and overlooked. Doubtless there are and will be individual instances of happy inconsistency, when such views of the efficacy of the baptismal rite are united with a truly spiritual and heavenly mind. Such cases occur even in the Church of Rome. And where there is

* If the hypothesis be adopted of a latent germ of spiritual life, deposited at baptism, but inert and inoperative until a subsequent conversion, to which some maintainers of this theory resort to get rid of obvious difficulties, then we must admit the existence of life which does not vivify, of light which does not shine, of grace that does not sanctify, of the indwelling of the Holy Spirit without producing holiness, of the tree being made good and yet the fruit remaining corrupt. Where is the syllable of Scripture to support a theory so extravagant?

not only the witness of conscience within, but that of an open Bible without, and the constant use of a fervent scriptural liturgy, it can not be but that the religion of many, who hold these exaggerated notions of sacramental grace, will be of a deeper tone and a more genuine character than their own system would produce or foster. But the tendency of the system toward a low standard of holiness and a lifeless formalism is inevitable. Let it prevail extensively in our Church, and we shall have a worldly sanctuary, and a people making parade of the form of godliness while denying the power thereof. The pure and elevated ethics of the Gospel will sink, as its distinguishing doctrines are obscured. There will be the easy and common transition from the communion-table to the ball-room, the theatre and the card-table. The hallowing of the Lord's day will be counted as Puritanical strictness. The worship of God in the family will become a rare thing. The supreme devotion of the young to the fashions and follies of the world will be deemed no impediment to their confirmation, and the holy ordinances of the Church will be intruded upon without rebuke, by those who are lovers of pleasures more than lovers of God. Missionary efforts will degenerate into mere proselytism; and if sea and land be compassed, it will be in the spirit of the Pharisees, rather than of the Apostles. No unprejudiced reader can fail to notice, in the prominent authors of this school, the depreciation of spiritual religion, the confounding of those evidences of a state of grace which the Scriptures, especially the Psalms and Epistles, make so prominent, with the vagaries and assumptions of enthusiasm. Let the cry be raised, "all the congregation are holy, every one of them, and the Lord is among them,"* and holiness will be soon reduced into something very different from that which shines with such heavenly lustre in the teaching of Paul and John.

Connected with this depreciation of the magnitude of the change effected by the Spirit, and this low standard of holiness, will be a fearful amount of self-deception. The multitude of undevout and carnally-minded persons who have received baptism will be taught to think themselves perfectly safe. Instead of being admonished by their spiritual guides to "examine themselves whether they be in the faith," to "prove their own selves," to ascertain whether "Jesus Christ be in them," or whether "they be reprobates;" they are assured that the great change indispensable to salvation has already taken place in their hearts. They are relieved from anxiety on this all-important point. They will feel no necessity of seeking God's renewing and converting grace. And in too many instances they will pass into eternity with a lie in their right hand, confident of their acceptance, until the awful truth burst upon them in the withering words, "I never knew you, depart from me all ye workers of iniquity."† Oh! let the teachers of this theology take heed that the blood of

* Numbers 16 : 3. † Matt. 7 : 23.

souls, deceived and lost for ever, be not found on their skirts.

10. Another tendency of this theory will be ultimately to dishonor and degrade the very ordinance which it aims to magnify. The fruits of exaggeration and unreality are always pernicious. Sooner or later comes the recoil. There is no surer way to bring a matter into contempt and suspicion, than to exalt it above measure. It is no benefit to the Church, the ministry, or the ordinances, to put them in the place of Christ and his Spirit, and to ascribe to them capacities which Scripture and reason do not warrant. The sober representations of the word of God can alone endure the test of time and experience. The only safety for aught pertaining to religion is truth and reality. Fictitious attributes may procure to a Christian ordinance, for a limited period, a sort of superstitious reverence; but when these borrowed garments are stripped off, there is great danger that the substance itself will be undervalued or discarded. To maintain the sacraments of the Gospel in their true position of privilege and sacred obligation, it is important to divest them of human exaggerations and misconceptions. To preserve the whole beautiful and perfect religion which the Lord hath revealed, and insure to the world its priceless benefits, it is of the utmost moment to adhere to the proportion of faith. Let each doctrine and each precept, each truth and each duty, occupy its proper place, as taught by Apostles and exhibited on the sacred page. And then all will point to Jesus, all will

converge in Christ crucified, and whatever be the immediate text or subject, men will be summoned to "behold the Lamb of God who taketh away the sins of the world." They will be brought to "believe in the Son of God, and believing, they will have life through his name."